THE SOUTH[

Nu-Wray Inn, Burnsville, North Carolina

COUNTRY INNS OF AMERICA

The Southeast

A GUIDE TO THE INNS OF FLORIDA, GEORGIA,
SOUTH CAROLINA, NORTH CAROLINA, VIRGINIA, AND WEST VIRGINIA

BY ROBERTA HOMAN GARDNER
AND PETER ANDREWS

PHOTOGRAPHED BY GEORGE W. GARDNER

DESIGNED BY ROBERT REID

HOLT, RINEHART AND WINSTON, *New York*

AN OWL BOOK

Cover photograph: River Forest Manor, Belhaven, N.C.
Frontispiece photograph: Glass collection, Nu-Wray Inn.
Back cover photograph: Wakulla Springs Lodge, Wakulla Springs, Florida.

Maps by Anthony St. Aubyn
Editing by Christine Timmons

Photographs on the following pages are used with permission from The Knapp Press, 5900 Wilshire Blvd, LA 90036, © 1978 by Knapp Communications Corporation: 1, 2, 12-23, 28-32, 52-55, 76-79, 82-87, 92-95.

Published by Holt, Rinehart and Winston, 383 Madison Avenue, New York, New York 10017.
Published simultaneously in Canada by Holt, Rinehart and Winston of Canada, Limited.

Library of Congress Cataloging in Publication Data

Gardner, Roberta Homan.
  The Southeast, a guide to the inns of Florida, Georgia, South Carolina, North Carolina, Virginia, and West Virginia.
    (Country inns of America)
    (An Owl book.)
    1. Hotels, taverns, etc.—Southern States—Directories. I. Andrews, Peter, 1931– . II. Title. III. Series.
  TX907.G343   647'.947501   81-20026
  ISBN 0-03-059178-3   AACR2

First Edition

10 9 8 7 6 5 4 3 2 1

A Robert Reid—Wieser & Wieser Production

Printed in the United States of America

ISBN 0-03-059178-3

THE INNS

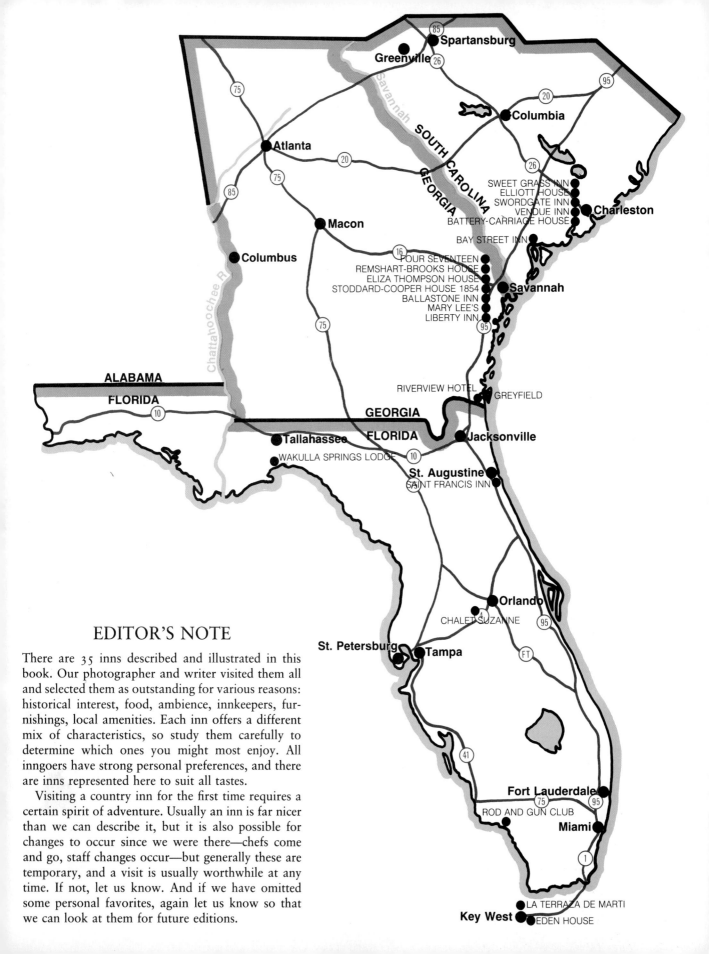

SOUTH CAROLINA

GEORGIA

Spartansburg

Greenville

Columbia

Atlanta

Macon

Columbus

SWEET GRASS INN
ELLIOTT HOUSE
SWORDGATE INN
VENDUE INN
BATTERY-CARRIAGE HOUSE

Charleston

BAY STREET INN

FOUR SEVENTEEN
REMSHART-BROOKS HOUSE
ELIZA THOMPSON HOUSE
STODDARD-COOPER HOUSE 1854
BALLASTONE INN
MARY LEE'S
LIBERTY INN

Savannah

ALABAMA

FLORIDA

GEORGIA

FLORIDA

RIVERVIEW HOTEL

GREYFIELD

Tallahassee

WAKULLA SPRINGS LODGE

Jacksonville

St. Augustine
SAINT FRANCIS INN

Orlando

CHALET SUZANNE

St. Petersburg

Tampa

Fort Lauderdale

ROD AND GUN CLUB

Miami

LA TERRAZA DE MARTI

Key West

EDEN HOUSE

EDITOR'S NOTE

There are 35 inns described and illustrated in this book. Our photographer and writer visited them all and selected them as outstanding for various reasons: historical interest, food, ambience, innkeepers, furnishings, local amenities. Each inn offers a different mix of characteristics, so study them carefully to determine which ones you might most enjoy. All inngoers have strong personal preferences, and there are inns represented here to suit all tastes.

Visiting a country inn for the first time requires a certain spirit of adventure. Usually an inn is far nicer than we can describe it, but it is also possible for changes to occur since we were there—chefs come and go, staff changes occur—but generally these are temporary, and a visit is usually worthwhile at any time. If not, let us know. And if we have omitted some personal favorites, again let us know so that we can look at them for future editions.

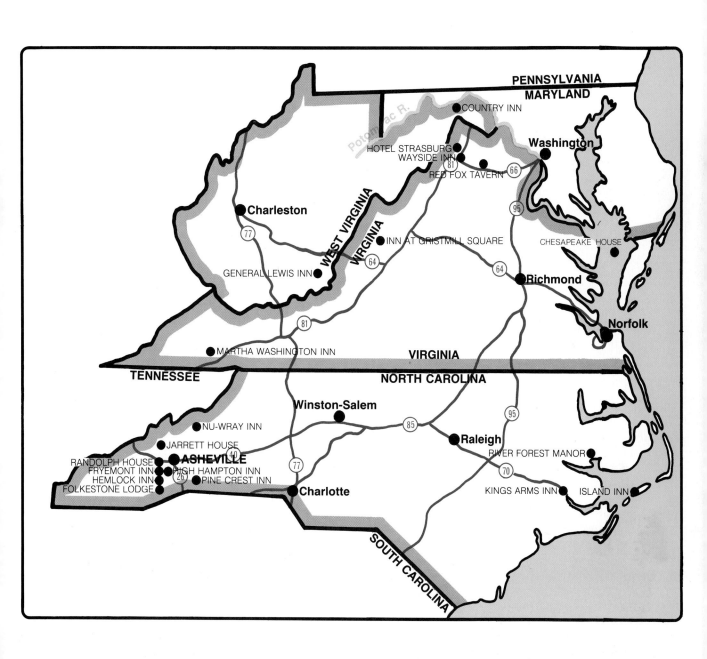

The ultimate in Key West exotica

"I was always taught that eating is the most important part of the day. No matter how bad your day is, eating can make it good," says Lawrence Formica, owner and proprietor of La Terraza De Marti. Larry's food, which sets local standards, truly can redeem the day. Brunch from 9 to 4 offers such delectables as oysters Florentine, Coquillages Tahitiens—a blend of oysters, clams, scallops, and tropical fruits bound together by homemade mayonnaise—and cold cucumber and avocado soup. Dinner, which is prix fixe and by reservation only, might feature a toothsome spiny lobster served with shrimp and crabmeat. Desserts are fabled and deservedly so.

Before booking into one of the attractive and comfortable guestrooms, take note. La Te Da, as it is known locally, is a party inn. Activity centers in the enclosed garden patio and bar which surrounds a palm-shrouded swimming pool. A multi-layered deck with second bar—and second kitchen serving fabulous fondue and Chinese food—is a great spot for people-watching. The general atmosphere at Le Te Da is very jet set and gay, but straight people are welcome and in evidence.

LA TERRAZA DE MARTI, 1125 Duval St., Key West, Fla. 33040; (305) 294-0344 or 294-5584; Lawrence Formica, Innkeeper. An 1892 Conch house (Conch being the name for Key West's original settlers and their offspring) with an enclosed central patio and swimming pool. Open year round. Eighteen air-conditioned rooms, 12 with semi-private baths and 6 with private baths; some with kitchenettes. Room rates range from $60 to $110. Restaurant with 2 kitchens, working on different menus, open to public and serving brunch and dinner 7 days a week in season; off season, brunch served daily and full dinner served weekends, with food also available in rooftop cocktail bar to supplement more limited off-season meal service. No children, no pets. All major credit cards accepted. Beaches, shopping, sailing, snorkeling, bicycling nearby. Local attractions include Conch Train, sunset at Mallory Square, Hemingway House, Audubon House.

DIRECTIONS: From Miami, take U.S.-1 to Key West, where U.S.-1 becomes first Roosevelt Blvd. and then Truman Ave. At corner of Truman Ave. and Duval St., turn left. La Te Da is 2 blocks on left.

Candlelit, outdoor dining is standard at "La Te Da," as the locals call the inn.

| *Key West* | # EDEN HOUSE | **FLORIDA** |

Key West at its most leisurely and seductive

The hot sun, humid air, and lazy pace of Key West as well as the local color—as often as not a deep tan promoted by scanty dress!—either appeal to the visitor or they do not. When Mike Eden ventured south from Flint, Michigan, a number of years ago, there was not the slightest doubt. He immediately fell in love with the westernmost of Florida's Keys and returned year after year until the purchase of the Eden House in 1975 enabled a permanent move.

Located on a sleepy side-street in Old Town, the 1924 two-story, white stucco boarding house is Key West's oldest hotel in continuous operation. The decor is simple and comfortable—white wicker, ceiling fans, and plants at every turn—and the atmosphere relaxed, quiet, and genial. The inn's restaurant, Rick's Cafe, is one of the best on the island and features a delectable local dish at breakfast, banana omelet with cream cheese and raisins, and excellent fresh fish at dinner.

The tempo on this island is leisurely and seductive, but for the energetic tourist there is much to see. Start with a grand tour of Key West on the famous Conch Train and make a point of visiting Ernest Hemingway's Home and Museum, and The Audubon House.

EDEN HOUSE, 1015 Fleming St., Key West, Fla. 23040; (305) 296-6868; Michael Eden, Innkeeper. Two-story, white stucco building with large overhanging porch in the city's Old Town. Open year round. Thirty-one guest rooms, 7 with private bath, 14 with semi-private bath, and 10 with bath down the hall; guest rooms have ceiling fans but no air-conditioning. Summer rates, $20–29 single; winter rates, $36 to $45 single; $5 for additional person. European plan. Restaurant, open to public, serves 3 meals 7 days a week in season, 2 meals 6 days a week out of season. No bar, but guests may bring beer or wine for dinner. Children under 16 not welcome, no pets. Visa and MasterCard accepted though not encouraged; discount for cash or check. Swimming and bike rental on premises; beaches, sailing, fishing, bird-watching, and nature sanctuaries nearby. Local attractions include the Conch Train, Hemingway House and Museum, and Audubon House.

DIRECTIONS: From Miami, take U.S.-1 to Key West, where U.S.-1 becomes first Roosevelt Blvd. and then Truman Ave. At intersection of Truman Ave. and Duval St., turn right on Duval and go to Fleming St. Turn right again and inn is 5 blocks down on the left.

Key West buildings have their own unique charm.

Right: The inn's interior reflects its sub-tropical location.

A funky jumble of turrets, minarets, and towers

Long before Walt Disney World came to Florida, there was the Chalet Suzanne. A funky jumble of turrets, minarets, towers and heaven knows what else, Chalet Suzanne is the sort of place where one would expect Dorothy to stop for lunch on her way to find the Wizard of Oz. It is a wonderfully wacky confusion of architectural and decorative styles, where nothing makes sense but everything works. The Swiss Dining Room is decorated in a profusion of Oriental tiles, and the Round Room is heptagonal. Huge, deep ashtrays are used as soup bowls, and doubtlessly there are some soup bowls that are being used as ashtrays.

As enchanting as it is, the Chalet Suzanne is much more than just an unusually strange inn with idiosyncratic furnishings. It is also a fine overnight accommodation, and a first-class restaurant with an international reputation for culinary excellence. *New York Times* critic Craig Claiborne placed Chalet Suzanne in the first rank of restaurants around the world.

Every place setting is different.

This gentle dreamland of a place is actually the result of more than forty years of hard work by a very tough-minded lady. In 1931, when America was in the grip of the Great Depression, Bertha Hinshaw was a widow with two children to look after, and no job. To support her family, she turned her home into a tiny restaurant and did all the cooking herself in a twelve-foot kitchen. Bertha had a natural eye for the business. Customers were willing to come long distances for Bertha's superb cooking, so the chatelaine added overnight guest facilities to allow them to stay even longer. Today, Chalet Suzanne has thirty guest rooms, and the restaurant seats 150 dinner guests.

Chalet Suzanne is now operated by Bertha's son Carl, his wife, Vita, and their children Tina and Eric. Carl and Vita were childhood sweethearts. They met on a school bus that was taking them to class in the fifth grade. Together, they carry on the tradition of fine service and gracious accommodation started by Bertha.

Left: The inn has its own private airstrip. OVERLEAF: Excellent food is served in startling surroundings—at left, in the Round Dining Room overlooking Lake Suzanne and, at right, in the Swiss Dining Room. The place setting shows a serving of Romaine soup. The following pages show the interior of the Governor Suite, left, above, and the exterior, right. Left, below, is the Orchid Room.

CHALET SUZANNE, P.O. Drawer AC, Lake Wales, Fla. 33853; (813) 676-1477; Carl and Vita Hinshaw, Innkeepers. A 30-room inn consisting of a series of small buildings on the shore of a private lake. Open all year. Double occupancy rates range from $38 to $60, suites, $50 to $80; $3 for additional person. Award-winning restaurant, open to public, serves breakfast, lunch, and dinner. From June to October restaurant closed Mondays. Bar open daily. Children welcome; pets $3 extra. All major credit cards accepted. Swimming pool.

DIRECTIONS: Forty mi. south of Disney World, off U.S.-27, halfway between Cypress Gardens and Bok Tower Garden. Watch for signs. Inn is located on Rte. 17A, 4 miles north of Lake Wales.

Everglades City ROD AND GUN LODGE

The dining room is paneled in cypress wood.

At the edge of a bountiful paradise

For nature lovers and sportsmen today, the Everglades is a bountiful paradise and a place of awesome beauty, offering sights unseen anywhere else in America and some of the best fishing in the world. The premier inn in this exotic country is the Rod and Gun Lodge, located less than a mile from the entrance to the Everglades National Park. A rambling, two-story house of white cypress, the lodge has been an exclusive sportsmen's hideaway for the last eighty years. Although most guests drive to the Rod and Gun Lodge from Miami or Fort Lauderdale, some fly their own planes to the nearby, 2,500-foot municipal landing strip.

Inside, it looks like a warm and comfortable hunting lodge, which it was until the Park Service outlawed all hunting in the Everglades twenty-five years ago. There is a cozy, cypress-paneled bar, decorated with stuffed fish, where anglers can gather for a cocktail in the evening and tell one another stories of what would have been the biggest catch of the season if it hadn't gotten away. Beyond the large hearth in the center of the lobby is a massive pool table with a stuffed alligator eight feet long suspended from the ceiling.

The dining room is the most formal part of the Rod and Gun Lodge. The walls are made of soft, pecky cypress, once considered a cheap local lumber, but now a highly prized wood. The room is furnished with comfortable club chairs, and chandeliers glow softly overhead. The restaurant is one of the most famous in southern Florida. Its menu consists of straightforward but beautifully prepared dishes with the emphasis on seafood.

Even the most incompetent angler should be able to bring some fresh fish home for dinner. The Rod and Gun Lodge is only a few yards away from its own marina on the Barron River and is directly across from part of the Ten Thousand Islands, a curved and crazy coastline that literally teems with fish. There are some fifty varieties within fifteen miles of the lodge, including grouper, bank fish, redfish, trout, snook and the sporting tarpon.

Left: Entrance to the dining room. OVERLEAF: Two views of the sumptuous, wood-paneled lobby. Following is a view of the inn and its marina.

ROD AND GUN LODGE, P.O. Drawer G, Everglades City, Fla. 33929; (813) 695-211; Martin Bowen, Innkeeper. A 17-room inn located near Everglades National Park. Open all year. Double occupancy rates range from $34 off season to $38 in season (Dec.-May); $4 for additional person, infants free. Restaurant, open to public, serves 3 meals daily; bar open daily. Children, pets welcome. No credit cards. Swimming pool; tennis courts, charter boats nearby.

DIRECTIONS: From Miami, take Rte. 41 west to State Hwy. 29; turn south on Hwy. 29 to get to Everglades City. Inn is 5 mi. south on Hwy. 29 on the right.

Wakulla Springs WAKULLA SPRINGS LODGE FLORIDA

An inn pet, the black bear "Freedom" gets its daily exercise.

An awesome sanctuary of exotic flora and fauna

On the list of must-see American wonders, Wakulla Springs ranks near the top. A 4000-acre enclosed wildlife sanctuary, surrounded by the Apalachicola National Forest, St. Mark's National Wildlife Refuge, and controlled forest land, Wakulla Springs offers an awesome catalogue of exotic flora and fauna, the largest and deepest natural spring in the world, and the Wakulla Springs Lodge.

Constructed in the early 1930s, this Spanish-style hostelry was built to last. In fact, so much Tennessee marble was used throughout that the interior feels more institutional than home-like. The lobby is open and spacious and contains a large stone fireplace; Mediterranean-style furniture; marble-topped tables; and a painted, beamed cypress ceiling. For a nice touch of kitsch, the main floor walls are lined with old-time, backlit Kodachromes of 1950s bathing beauties; and nearby stands a case with a stuffed 200-year-old, 650-pound alligator—Old Joe, who lived his long life in the spring across from the hotel. Flanking the lobby are the soda parlor/gift shop, with a sixty-foot marble soda fountain, and the formal dining room, whose dining chairs are the most comfortable imaginable—heavily padded rockers with arms. Specialties from the kitchen include tender, moist pan-fried chicken, prime rib of beef, toothsome navy bean soup, and homemade pecan pie. Possibly the finest culinary treats of all are tea and coffee made from Wakulla Springs water. Incredibly good!

But the real reason to stay at the hotel is to commune with the spring and its abundant wildlife. Two boat rides—a glassbottomed sweep over the spring and a jungle cruise down river—and several hiking trails offer access to this wild and mysterious tract. Of special interest are the boat guides, who recount the legend of the spring and its inhabitants in a sing-song chant reminiscent of a black gospel preacher's stylized speech. The water is so clear you can see the bottom at its deepest point—185 feet! In the springs there is much to be seen—Henry, the pole-vaulting fish; several giant mastodon bones; and lots of beautiful species of fish. Wakulla Springs is also home to an impressive array of wildlife and rare birds. Guests on the flat-bottom riverboat tour might see turtles, alligators, deer, bear, turkey, a large wading bird called a limpkin that is nearly extinct, anhingas, pied-billed grebes, widgeons, osprey, heron, and much more.

And finally after a good meal and a visit with springs and river, it is time for a swim in the pellucid waters to muse, perhaps, on the days when Ponce de León gazed by the hour into the springs' translucent depths, thinking that he had finally found the fountain of youth.

Left: Scenes on the Jungle Cruise down the Wakulla River. Above, an Anhinga, perched on the roots of a Cypress, drying its wings. Below, an alligator sunning on the river bank.

WAKULLA SPRINGS LODGE, 1 Spring Dr., Wakulla Springs, Fla. 32305; (904) 640-7011; Joe R. Wilkie, Innkeeper. A spacious, Spanish-style lodge built in the stunning setting of a 4000-acre enclosed wildlife sanctuary that boasts the world's largest and deepest natural springs and an awesome array of exotic flora and fauna. Open year round. Twenty-five rooms, each with private bath with both tub and shower. Room rates $23 to $26.50 single, $27.50 to $31 double, $37.50 to $44 two luxury waterfront rooms; $3.50 additional adults, $2.25 additional children. European plan. Dining room, open to public, serves 3 meals daily 7 days a week. No bar or lounge; guests may bring wine or beer for dinner. Children welcome, no pets. MasterCard and Visa accepted. Guided boat tours of river and springs, swimming, hiking; Tallahassee, Florida's capital, nearby.

DIRECTIONS: From Tallahassee, take Hwy. 319 south to Rte. 61 and follow signs to Wakulla Springs and lodge.

St. Augustine | # ST. FRANCIS INN | **FLORIDA**

A striking combination of Spanish-Victorian

The St. Francis Inn is the only historic site in St. Augustine that offers lodgings, allowing guests to share intimately in the life of this richly textured city—the oldest in North America.

Built in 1791 of coquina—a limestone formed of broken shells and coral—the structure has since been occupied continuously, alternately as a private residence and guesthouse. The inn reveals its lineage in a striking combination of Spanish lines and Victorian embellishments; among the latter are a tongue-in-groove ceiling and an ornate fireplace in the parlor. Today the inn is owned and operated by Elizabeth and Charles Davis, who moved from Ohio to St. Augustine to "retire." Actually, the inn is Elizabeth's bailiwick and is filled with antiques and comfortable furnishings that she has collected over the years.

From St. George Street, guests enter through an iron gate and are at once transported to a lush garden courtyard filled with bougainvillea, jasmine, banana trees, and a bubbling fountain. From here they can sit and rock the day away under a slow-moving porch paddle fan, go for a dip in the secluded swimming pool, or browse through Elizabeth's antique shop just inside the inn. The central staircase leads up to the second-floor guest rooms past a gallery of paintings of the inn and St. Augustine—creations by former guests and several local artists. The inn houses throughout a large collection of paintings and interesting *objets*.

The sitting room.

Travelers on extended vacations welcome the fact that most rooms contain kitchenettes, allowing for a blessed break from restaurant dining. And though several of the rooms are in need of renovation and redecoration, all are quite comfortable. Across the courtyard sits a two-story cottage—once slave quarters—which have been completely renovated and may be rented for a night or for extended stays.

A tour of St. Augustine might begin with a ride on the sightseeing train, which takes in all the points of historical interest. Several of the most interesting stops include San Agustin Antiguo, an eighteenth-century restored-and-working village; Castillo de San Marcos, built circa 1672 and the oldest masonry fortification in the United States; and "The Oldest House," which was constructed in 1702 and is just two doors from the inn.

Left: Industrialist Henry Flagler developed Florida as a winter playground and Saint Augustine was a beneficiary of grand parks and buildings. A former Flagler hotel is now the Lightner museum shown here.

ST. FRANCIS INN, 279 St. George St., St. Augustine, Fla. 32084; (904) 824-6068; Elizabeth H. Davis, Innkeeper. Spanish colonial, coquina structure with added slate mansard roof. Open year round. Seven guest rooms, 5 with kitchenettes, and 1 cottage next to inn in garden; each room has private bath, but 2 have non-attached private baths down the hall. Room rates $20 to $40, cottage $60; special weekly and monthly rates; additional person in room $5. No dining room, no bar. Children welcome, no pets. No credit cards. Antique shop on premises. Historic St. Augustine offers wealth of sights to see, including Fountain of Youth, Zorayda Castle, San Augustin Antiguo, Castillo De San Marcos, and the oldest house and oldest schoolhouse in the U.S.; Marineland, Alligator Farm, Lightner Museum nearby.

DIRECTIONS: From south or north, take U.S.-1 to St. Augustine; at sign for business district at intersection of U.S.-1 and King St., turn left (east) on King St. and go to 4th traffic light; turn right (south) on St. George St., and inn is 2 blocks away.

Cumberland Island # GREYFIELD INN

Carnegie heirlooms amid unspoiled wilderness

The Greyfield Inn is like no other place in America. Half the time, it can't be reached by telephone, and when people write ahead for reservations, as often as not they receive instead a request for references. When they are finally accepted as guests, they will find that the Greyfield Inn is almost impossible to get to—a boat and a chartered airplane are the only means. Once they arrive at Greyfield, if the guests are looking for traditional resort activities, they will find there is practically nothing to do. There are no golf courses nearby, no tennis courts on the property and no swimming pool. Yet despite all this, or perhaps because of it, Greyfield is one of the most memorable country inns on the eastern seaboard. What guests do find when they come to Greyfield is a gracious, richly appointed private home, fine food and one of the few patches of completely unspoiled wilderness left in America.

Greyfield was built around the turn of the century as the island hideaway of Thomas Carnegie, Andrew's brother. It was the Carnegie home for generations and is still owned by Lucy Ferguson, Thomas's granddaughter.

Guests are ushered into a fine old home. The living room is paneled in dark wood offset with bright, rustic colors. While a fire crackles on the oversized hearth, guests are free to have a cup of tea in one of the Morris chairs or just lounge around on the sofa, reading a book from the Carnegies' library just down the hall. Greyfield is filled with family memorabilia: stacks of old photograph albums of the Carnegies at play in the early part of the twentieth century; hundreds of varieties of seashells gathered during family excursions over the island; and a shelf full of sports trophies from long-forgotten country club tournaments.

A major event at Greyfield is dinner, served buffet-style from a huge mahogany sideboard in the main dining room. There is no permanent chef; so the food varies from week to week, as various local cooks

The house is unaltered and is maintained much as it was when the Carnegies lived there.

come over from the mainland to prepare their specialties—rack of lamb, one of the many local game birds or any of a variety of regional fish. The special treat of the house is roast suckling pig.

The upstairs rooms vary greatly, from relatively small to one baronial sleeping chamber fitted out with a massive bed that is covered with the same white spread Mrs. Ferguson had as a child.

Cumberland Island itself is a nature lover's paradise. Hiking, shelling, beachcombing and birdwatching are the staple activities at Greyfield. As they say on the island, "The only recreational director here is Mother Nature."

GREYFIELD INN, Drawer B, Fernandina Beach, Fl. 32034; (904) 356-9509; reservations office in Fernandina—call Karen Chaplin, (904) 356-9509. Mrs. Lucy Ferguson and her 3 grandchildren, Mitty, Andy and Janet, Innkeepers. An 8-room inn with 2 cottages, located on Cumberland Island, Georgia. Open all year. Rates $75 per day per person including all meals, served buffet style. Semi-private baths. Children welcome at special rates and discounts, depending on age. Self-service bar, closed Sundays. MasterCard and Visa accepted. Nature walks arranged by inn.

DIRECTIONS: Private inn ferry from Fernandina Beach; obtain schedule from reservations office. Jack's Helicopter Service from Jacksonville airport lands at inn. Private planes can land on island airstrip 3½ miles from inn; phone ahead to inn to be met. Park Service boats from St. Marys, Georgia; schedules from reservations office.

Left: A corner of the living room. OVERLEAF: Woody vines thread the live oaks near the entrance to Greyfield.

RIVERVIEW HOTEL

St. Marys   **GEORGIA**

Unpretentious charm on the waterfront

"Frontier spartan." "Super, charming, unspoiled." "Very peaceful—it grows on you." So reads a sampling of inscriptions from the Riverview Hotel's guestbook, attesting to the unpretentious charm of this inn. Built in 1916 on the waterfront of St. Marys, the Riverview was long owned and operated by three great-aunts and then the parents of present innkeeper Jerry Brandon. The hotel is a two-story, tabby stuccoed structure, whose decor is comfortable but simple. Not to be missed in the lobby are some of the original "Wash Tubbs" comic strips from the 1930s in which cartoonist and long-time Riverview guest Roy Crane made the inn famous. In Seagle's, the inn's restaurant, be sure to sample some of the fresh seafood and delicious pecan pie for dessert.

St. Marys, second oldest town in the U.S., offers the visitor an interesting stroll among its historic buildings and fascinating old cemetery as well as access by ferry—just across the street from the hotel—to Cumberland Island National Seashore and Greyfield Inn.

RIVERVIEW HOTEL, 105 Osborne St., St. Marys, Ga. 31558; (912) 882-3242; Jerry and Sara Brandon, Innkeepers. A 2-story, stuccoed structure, with a tabby of seashells pressed into the stucco, that overlooks the river and downtown St. Marys. Open year round. Eighteen guest rooms, including 1 2-room suite; each room has private bath (2 have showers only). Room rates $23 single, $27 double; $4 for additional person. Children under 12 free. Restaurant, open to public, serves 3 meals a day 6 days a week; closed Sun. and no lunch served on Sat. Bar on premises. Children welcome, no pets. Visa, MasterCard, American Express accepted. Rocking chairs on second-floor porch constitute recreational facilities on premises; fishing, hunting, hiking on Cumberland Island; Okeefenokee Swamp, historical buildings and fascinating old cemetery nearby.

DIRECTIONS: From Jacksonville, Fla., take I-95 north to St. Marys Rd. Exit (first exit in Ga.); travel east approximately 3 mi. to Hwy. 40. Turn right on Hwy. 40 and drive approximately 6 mi. Hotel is at dead end of Hwy. 40. From Atlanta, Ga., take Hwy. 40 or take I-95 to Exit 2 (Hwy. 40 exit); follow sign to St. Marys and turn left onto Hwy. 40. Hotel is at end of Hwy. 40.

Left: Greyfield's library, which contains a number of signed first editions. For those heading for Greyfield, St. Marys is the stopping off place from where the boat leaves.

The second floor balcony overlooks St. Marys River.

FOUR SEVENTEEN—THE HASLAM-FORT HOUSE
STODDARD-COOPER HOUSE 1854
MARY LEE'S GUEST ACCOMMODATIONS
LIBERTY INN
REMSHART-BROOKS HOUSE

Bed and breakfast in historic Savannah

Historic Savannah, two and one-half square miles of protected landmark territory, is among the fairest of American cities. For newcomers it is a wonderful surprise to find a graceful combination of attractive elements from other cities and places; mansions and townhouses reminiscent of Boston or New York; twenty meticulously tended town squares that rival Washington, D.C., or even Paris, in auspicious city planning; tropical palms and giant agave shaded by

Left: One of the bedrooms in Four Seventeen's sumptuous apartment.

moss-draped oaks; New Orleans-style ironwork; and an active riverfront that combines original cobblestones and wharf-front brokerage houses with contemporary shops and restaurants. In such a place as this, private residences seem to hold intriguing secrets. In Savannah the vistor may enter.

First to be contacted is MARY LEE whose private GUEST ACCOMMODATIONS were the first in Savannah. A city native and vivacious ball of fire, Mary offers three apartments—one in the slave quarters on the ground floor of her tabby-covered townhouse and two in the coachhouse just behind the enclosed garden courtyard. A dedicated collector of antiques and great "junk," she has furnished each apartment with a variety of colorful rugs, quilts, china, and comfortable furniture. Mary's intention is to make people feel as if they are in their own homes, and through a blend

The Haslam-Fort House.

A Liberty Inn guest room.

of atmosphere and fine spirit she succeeds admirably.

Mary's friend Alan Fort opened the ground floor of his historic townhouse, FOUR SEVENTEEN, as one luxurious apartment. Alan, a well-traveled and urbane host, was inspired by an inn in Chur, Switzerland, and from that example set out to create an atmosphere where Americans and Europeans alike could feel completely at home. Stenciled wallpaper, brass and spool bedsteads, and lots of wonderful American antiques played against glowing heart pine floors and Savannah grey brick, all unite in a symphony of texture and colors—which, by the way, are of the historic Savannah variety and feature syllabub white, Habersham's vest blue, and peach leather.

Both Mary and Alan work in a loose cooperative with three other wonderful private homes; the LIBERTY INN, The STODDARD-COOPER HOUSE, and the REMSHART-BROOKS HOUSE. Each is a historic Savannah home with a pedigree as long as your arm, and all are well situated for exploring the glories of the city. The LIBERTY offers a clutch of apartments complete with cable television, a hidden washer-dryer in each, and a jacuzzi in the garden. Both the REMSHART-BROOKS and STODDARD-COOPER have converted their ground floor slave quarters into magnificently spacious apartments and, like the rest, have full, working kitchens that are stocked with the fixings for a continental breakfast. Several supply fresh fruit and a variety of scrumptious pastries, and there might even be a box of fresh eggs ready to be transformed into a full and sumptuous repast.

MARY LEE, GUEST ACCOMMODATIONS, 117 E. Jones, Box 607, Savannah, Ga. 31402; (912) 232-0891 or 236-7101; Mary Lee, Innkeeper. Federal-style townhouse, built in 1854. Open year round. Three full apartments; $50 per unit. No bar. Children welcome, pets not encouraged. No credit cards. Nearby shops, restaurants, museums, and points of historic interest.

FOUR SEVENTEEN—THE HASLAM-FORT HOUSE, 417 E. Charlton St., Savannah, Ga., 31401; (912) 233-6380; Alan Fort, Innkeeper. Italianate brick townhouse, built in 1872. Open year round. One full suite with fireplace, 2 bedrooms, and full kitchen; private off-street parking. Rates $75 per couple, $125 for 2 couples or family of 4; $20 for each additional person, no charge for children under 12. Coffee, tea, juice, soft drinks, pastry provided. No bar. Children welcome, pets not encouraged. No credit cards. Side yard; board games, television, radio provided.

THE STODDARD-COOPER HOUSE, 19 W. Perry St., Savannah, Ga. 31401; (912) 233-6809 or 234-5305; David and Barbara Hershey, Innkeepers. Georgian townhouse built in

Living room of the apartment in the Stoddard-Cooper House.

1854. Open year round. One apartment with living room and 2 bedrooms; $68 to $98, depending on number of guests, includes provisions for a continental breakfast that guests fix themselves. No bar. Children welcome; crib available and babysitting can be arranged. No pets. No credit cards. Bicycles, private garden, barbecue grill on premises.

REMSHART-BROOKS HOUSE, 106 W. Jones St., Savannah, Ga. 31401; (912) 236-4337; Charles and Martha Brooks, Innkeepers. Historic rowhouse built in 1854. Open year round. Two-room suite with 2 working fireplaces, bath, fully equipped kitchen, and private parking; can accommodate 2 couples. $50 rate includes provisions for continental breakfast that guests prepare themselves. No bar. Children welcome, no pets. Visa, MasterCard accepted. Walled courtyard on premises.

LIBERTY INN, 128 W. Liberty St., Savannah, Ga. 31401; (912) 233-1007; Frank and Janie Harris, Innkeepers. Clapboard colonial home built in 1834. Open year round. Four suites with kitchenettes: 2-room suite $65 per couple, $5 each additional person; 3-room suite $100 for 4 people; includes provisions for fixing continental breakfast. Reservations suggested. No bar. Children welcome, no pets. American Express, MasterCard, Visa accepted. Spa with whirlpool hot tub, barbecue grill on premises.

DIRECTIONS: Take I-16 east to the last exit (Exit 37-B/Montgomery St.) and Montgomery St. to Liberty St. and the historic district. Call innkeepers for specific directions to each inn.

Mary Lee's

One of Mary Lee's guest rooms in the slave quarters.

Savannah's past recreated in exquisite detail

Every cosmopolitan city should have a Ballastone Inn. Intimate, stylish, and complete with a concierge who is anxious to serve, the Ballastone is more a polished hotel than a home-grown "country" inn.

Guests enter the Ballastone through heavy double doors, made elegant by panes of etched glass, and cross the vestibule's marble floor. At the edge of a rich tapestry rug awaits the concierge, the soft light of a green-glass study lamp playing over his antique desk. Flanking the reception area are a lovely Victorian staircase, embellished with twisted spindles and an ornate *torchère* on the newel post, and the guest lounge. The latter is a rich combination of

Left: The lounge with Victorian setee and Cotton Exchange wallpaper.

bamboo, marble, and crystal, wrapped in "stained glass"—a fabric wall covering adapted from a stained glass window found in Savannah's historic Cotton Exchange. It is here that guests receive a complimentary cocktail, savory benne wafers, and perhaps a deviled crab snack.

The entire inn, including all nineteen guestrooms, is decorated in wallpaper, paint, fabric, and rugs from Scalamandre's Savannah Collection, a decorator's line created from the designs found on shards of china, wallpaper scraps, and bits of fabric discovered from Savannah's Victorian past. The creator of the line is a local artist who was given carte blanche to make the Ballastone a complete showcase.

Therefore each room is distinctly different from the rest and each has its own name: China Trade, Scarborough Fair, Gazebo, and Peach Leather, to name a few. Besides the rich use of color, every room contains either a king- or queen-size bed that has a canopy or four-poster rice or wicker bedstead; wooden stools to aid ascent into tall beds; fresh fruits and flowers; and, at evening turn-down, a snifter of brandy, a praline, and a poem. To top it all off,

The staircase, with twisted spindle railings.

bathrooms are provided with Dior terrycloth bath-robes.

Continental breakfast arrives at a designated hour. Awaken to muffins and fancy fruit breads, fresh fruit, juice, and your favorite steaming beverage; and reflect in blissful luxury upon the truth of the bedside poem:

"Whoe'er has travel'd life's dull round
What e'er his various tours has been
May sigh to think how oft he found
His warmest welcome at Inn."

BALLASTONE INN, 14 E. Oglethorpe Ave., Savannah, Ga. 31401; (912) 236-1484; Tarby Bryant, Innkeeper; Brad Holloway, Manager. Elegant Victorian townhouse built in 1835 provides a gracious setting for this inn that pays heed to the amenities. Open year round. Nineteen rooms, each with private bath and either king- or queen-sized bed. Room rates single from $60, double from $77, master rooms from $137; $20 for extra person. Rates include continental breakfast, daily newspapers, and complimentary fruit and liqueur. No dining room. Lounge serving liquor, open to guests only. Children welcome, no pets. American Express, Visa, MasterCard accepted. Backgammon, cards, chess in lobby.

DIRECTIONS: Take I-16 east to last exit (Exit 37-B/Montgomery St.); stay on Montgomery and turn right at Oglethorpe. At 2nd stoplight go around median to inn.

The Savannah has matching queen sized four poster beds.

Right: The elegant Victoria with Chinese rug.

Savannah ELIZA THOMPSON HOUSE

From stately townhouse to sumptuous inn

One of Savannah's stateliest townhouses, the Eliza Thompson House has a history. Constructed in 1847, it was home for the vivacious, red-headed widow, Eliza Thompson, and her seven children. Nine parts determination and one part inspiration, Eliza made the best of turbulent wartimes by selling corncakes to Union soldiers during Sherman's occupation, a delicacy baked in her huge kitchen hearth. Meanwhile, Eliza's daughter Georgia, operated a 'proper school' for young ladies in the spacious home.

Today the Eliza Thompson House offers genial hospitality to wayfarers, thanks to Jim and Laurie Widman, who spent endless hours meticulously restoring the entire building, inside and out. The inn boasts of thirteen working fireplaces—including one in a bathroom and the famous kitchen hearth which now warms a guest room—and one of the largest and loveliest private gardens in the historic district. Here, three fountains, including a copper 'lily pad' which is an Ivan Bailey masterwork, red brick herringbone pavement, and lush vegetation create a

tranquil atmosphere. If the weather turns inclement one need not give up the pleasures of the garden, for a protected loggia insures comfort from the elements.

Inside, a formal reception parlor is the scene of late afternoon relaxation or lively conversation. Furnished with Sheraton and Hepplewhite antiques and graced with a mahogany and cypress fireplace, gilt pier glass, Chinese vases, and a Georgian brass chandelier, the parlor offers an 'honor system' bar for guests and their party. Each bedroom is strikingly painted in hues chosen from the 'historic Savannah' palette, colors accented by a large collection of *Vanity Fair*'s satirical Spy prints. Bedsteads are either antique—and include Lauri's grandmother's ornate mahogany bridal bed—or fluted four-posters made especially for the inn. Such amenities as soaps bedded in handwoven baskets and a Continental breakfast of fresh croissants and Eliza's recipe for corncakes, served on fine silver and the inn's own china, are touches that create a luxurious atmosphere and fond memories. The Widman's presence adds the final touch of grace as they proffer the best of Southern hospitality.

All this and much more insure that Eliza Thompson's home has a future to surpass its history.

ELIZA THOMPSON HOUSE, 5 W. Jones St., Savannah, Georgia 31401; (912) 236-3620; Laurie and Jim Widman, Innkeepers. A 17-room Federalist-style townhouse in the heart of historic Savannah. Three suites include hideaway kitchens. The walled garden is one of Savannah's finest. Open all year. Rates available upon request. Continental breakfast included in tariff; 'honor system' bar available to inn guests. No pets, no credit cards. Historic Savannah offers a bounty of pastimes.

DIRECTIONS: Take I-16 to its termination, which is Montgomery St. exit. At corner of Montgomery and Liberty St. turn right, onto Liberty. Drive to Whitaker St. and turn right onto Whitaker. Drive three blocks to Jones St. and turn left. Inn is in first block, on the right.

The whole inn is newly decorated: at *left* is an elegant sitting room and *above*, a beautiful, sunlit guest room.

BAY STREET INN

Beaufort   **SOUTH CAROLINA**

An antebellum mansion in a picturesque port

If your vision of the perfect southern inn vacation includes a stay at a gracious plantation-style mansion, the Bay Street Inn should be on your itinerary. The Lewis Reeve Sams house, built on the banks of the Beaufort River in 1852, was for sale just as Terry and David Murray were searching for an inn. Both were suffering from overwork and undersatisfaction in Phoenix, where David was an engineer and Terry was director of the State Planning Office; having always enjoyed vacationing at inns around the country, they decided that innkeeping would be a fine new career. Scouring the East Coast from Savannah to Charleston, they discovered the picturesque port of Beaufort—pronounced BEW-fert by its 9,000 inhabitants; they were struck by its impressive collection of antebellum mansions preserved from Civil War destruction and its palm-lined river, part of the Intracoastal Waterway, where boats sail past from the Atlantic to the town's sheltered harbor and dolphins swim in unison.

The inn's manicured lawn, filled with magnolias, crepe myrtle, azaleas, and two poinsettas said to have been planted by J. R. Poinsett himself, is enclosed by a white picket fence. A small brass plate at the gate quietly announces the Bay Street Inn. Through this gate and up the age-worn, white marble staircase, guests enter the foyer. The parlor on the right is elegantly furnished in classic French furniture set off by a dramatic black marble fireplace and brocade wallpaper. Up the broad, heart pine staircase, each lovely bedroom has a distinct character. One contains a spectacular Parisian bedstead of butternut and inlaid yew; another features a stately mahogany bed; a third houses a French vanity, wardrobe, and Louis XVI cane bed. All are supplied with a generous basket of fresh fruit and a carafe of sherry to be sipped from antique crystal glasses.

A hearty breakfast is prepared daily by Terry and served on fine china in the dining room. Situated at the back of the house, the dining room features large windows surveying the lawn and a massive circular table covered with a cloth of rich burgundy splashed

Left: The light and inviting dining room. OVERLEAF: The inn seen from the Beaufort River.

The library.

with golden day lilies. A crystal chandelier casts rainbow light about the room; and cushioned, ladder-back chairs combine with a decorative white Victorian fireplace, cabinets displaying a wonderful collection of china and silver, and potted tree and plants to create a light, cheerful atmosphere.

BAY STREET INN, 601 Bay St., Beaufort (pronounced BEW-fert), S.C. 29902; (803) 524-7720; Terry and David Murray, Innkeepers. Greek Revival-style frame house with graceful double verandas and an elegant interior that once belonged to one of Beaufort's most prominent families; situated in an historic community that offers the history buff a heyday and the fatigued traveler a quiet respite. Open year round. Five guest rooms; each has private bath, 2 with tub only, 3 with shower only. Room rates $43 to $55 single, $48 to $60 double; rates include continental breakfast, served in the dining room, garden, or porch. No meal service other than breakfast. No bar, but guests may bring their own liquor. Inn is not suitable for children, no pets. MasterCard, Visa accepted. Bicycles on premises for sight-seeing in Beaufort; historic district, harbor, antique shops, Hunting Island beach, golf, tennis, swimming all nearby.

DIRECTIONS: From Savannah, take I-95 north to Exit 8 (Rd. 88) and follow signs to Beaufort on Hwy. 170. From Hwy. 170, take Hwy. 21 (at McDonalds); turn right and follow to Bay St. and turn left. Inn is third house. From Charleston, take Hwy. 17 south to Hwy. 21 and follow signs to Beaufort. Stay on Hwy. 21 until Bay St., where you turn left and inn is third house.

Charleston

SWEET GRASS INN
VENDUE INN
BATTERY-CARRIAGE HOUSE
ELLIOT HOUSE

SOUTH CAROLINA

Four Charleston inns offer Southern hospitality

Charleston, essence of Old South romance and gentility. An American jewel whose architecture dates back to the original colonies and whose culture and sophistication reflect the era when it was known as "Little London." Delicious food, fascinating history, architectural treasures gracing beautifully appointed

Left: Sweetgrass Inn rooftop patio.

avenues and parks, flowers and baskets made of native sweet grass sold by street vendors, the Spoleto Festival, the City Market. Charleston's charms are all the more satisfying when your pied-à-terre is an inn nestled in the heart of the historic district.

Evelyn and Morton Needle wanted their visiting guests to be comfortably accommodated and so began the VENDUE INN, an early nineteenth-century warehouse converted into an elegant and intimate hotel. Each room is named for a prominent South Carolinian and comes complete with a concise biography. Evelyn took care to decorate the rooms individually, using classic Charleston reproduction furniture and historic colors. Every afternoon complimentary wine and cheese are served in the garden room, an event made

A Sweetgrass Inn guest room.

Elliot House breakfast patio.

especially pleasant by frequent musicales. A complimentary continental breakfast is served daily, and service by the staff is well informed and cordial. Several blocks away is the VENDUE HOUSE, another restored historic building owned by the Needles which houses suites and their antique shop and which caters to families or visitors planning extended stays.

Just next door, another nineteenth-century warehouse was born again—this time as the SWEET GRASS INN. Managed with infectious Southern charm by Susan Bigbie, the inn is decorated "country style." Rooms feature full, ruffled, white tie-back curtains; gleaming heart pine floors; colorful coverlets which change seasonally; and fresh fruits and flowers. The full breakfast, which is served each morning at an antique table in the dining room, can be enjoyed, weather permitting, on a wonderful rooftop patio. From this vantage, guests can savor the charm of Charleston's rooftops as well as the unimpeded view of Fort Sumter in the harbor.

At the tip of the Battery, across from White Point Garden and the harbor, the house at 20 South Battery stands in awesome grandeur. Built in 1845, the carriage house and ground floor now form the BAT-TERY-CARRIAGE HOUSE. Through ornate iron gates and past two sentry lions, guests enter the inn proper with its ironwork balcony and verdant lawn of grand dimensions. Owners Frank and Becky Gay restored the rooms in elegant style complete with tester and half-tester beds, monogrammed coverlets, and hidden kitchenettes supplied with a complimentary bottle of wine, which is replenished, if needed, each day of your stay. Morning is greeted by a silver tray laden with coffee, muffins and jelly, and a generous slab of Benedict cheesecake baked by Frank's Aunt Lee. So great was the demand for a room at the inn that the Gays bought another building in the historic district, refurbished the existing structure—built circa 1860—and rebuilt the old slave quarters area. Therefore, at the ELLIOT HOUSE guests have a choice between the historic building with its charming irregularities or the new structure, both of which are furnished with historic Charleston reproductions. The entire inn surrounds a brick courtyard with an inviting sunken jacuzzi as centerpiece. As at the Battery-Carriage, a complimentary bottle of wine is supplied with each room, and Benedict cheesecake arrives on the morning breakfast tray.

The Vendue Inn.

BATTERY-CARRIAGE HOUSE, 20 S. Battery, Charleston, S.C. 29401; (803) 723-9881; Kathy Riopel, Manager. Greek Revival mansion with elegantly restored carriage house, set in an enclosed garden. Open year round. Ten rooms, each with private bath and fully equipped, concealed kitchenette. Room rates $53 to $64 single, $64 to $75 double; includes continental breakfast and complimentary bottle of wine. No restaurant or bar, but room service for wine and beer available. Children welcome, no pets. Visa, MasterCard, American Express accepted. Free bicycles for guests.

ELLIOT HOUSE, 78 Queen St., Charleston, S.C. 29401; (803) 723-1855; LeRoy Benedict, Manager. Restored private residence in historic district, with brick courtyard and jacuzzi pool. Open year round. Twenty-six rooms, each with private bath. Room rates $55 to $66 single, $71 to $94 double; includes continental breakfast and complimentary bottle of wine. No bar or restaurant, but room service available for beer and wine. Children welcome, no pets. Visa, MasterCard, American Express accepted. Free bicycles for touring Charleston.

DIRECTIONS: From I-95 take I-26 into Charleston. Exit on Hwy. 17N and then turn right on East Bay St. For Vendue and Sweet Grass, drive approximately 1½ mi. to Vendue Range (2 blocks past market area). For Elliot House, drive down East Bay to Queen St.; inn is on Queen St. across Meeting St., just behind Mills House Hotel. For Battery-Carriage House, take East Bay to Battery St.; inn is across from park.

VENDUE INN, 19 Vendue Range, Charleston, S.C. 29401; (803) 577-7970; VENDUE HOUSE, 9 Queen St., Charleston, S.C. 29401; (803) 577-5462; Evelyn and Morton Needle, Innkeepers. Inn is converted commercial building, built c. 1800, with Georgian touches; house, two blocks away, is a restored antebellum mansion, dating to 1814. Both open year round. Inn: 18 rooms; house: 5 suites or 10 rooms; all with private baths. Room rates $63 to $68 single, $68 to $77 double; suites $99 to $142; includes continental breakfast and complimentary wine and cheese hour. No restaurant or bar, but complete room service available. Children welcome, no pets. All major credit cards, except Diners Club, accepted. Bicycles furnished for touring historic Charleston.

SWEET GRASS INN, 23 Vendue Range, Charleston, S.C 29401; (803) 723-9980; Susan Bigbie, Innkeeper. Renovated commercial warehouse, built around 1800, features flat facade and Federal fan windows. Open year round. Eight guestrooms, including 1 suite; all have private bath with shower and tub. Rates $55 single, $60 to $80 double; $10 for additional person, $5 for infants (crib free), includes full breakfast. Dining room for inn guests serves breakfast only; no bar. Children welcome, no pets. No credit cards accepted. Free bicycles for touring the area.

The Battery-Carriage House.

SWORDGATE INN

Opulent decor and gracious charm

The Swordgate Inn, a tiny little bandbox of a place situated in the heart of Charleston's historic district, is a nineteenth-century guest house with a score of charming grace notes.

The four bedrooms on the ground floor have the graciousness of a century-old establishment, offset by vibrant modern color coordination and accessories. The rooms are filled with attractive linens, ruffled pillows, coverlets in bright fabrics and upholstered chairs. The baths have thick towels in lime and mint green. The top-floor bedroom is the most elegant. Its high ceiling accommodates a lofty, four-poster bed with a hand-crocheted canopy of incredible intricacy made entirely of tobacco tying threads. There is also a lovely, formal fireplace with a sterling silver poker.

The dining area is tiny, just four tables with green-and-white checked tablecloths in a narrow room that sometimes doubles as an office. When the weather is accommodating, as it often is, everyone goes out on the patio, with its wrought-iron tables and garden chairs, and eats under the morning sun.

Although the inn is quite small, there are two opulent rooms on the second floor—a formal dining room, and a magnificent ballroom that is a regular stop on the annual Charleston House Tours. In 1977, the Preservation Society of Charleston held a candlelit ceremony in the gilded ballroom, where five musicians performed on recorders for some five hundred visitors. In the daytime, the sun streams through the twelve-

The crocheted string canopy made from tobacco tying cord.

foot windows, and a gigantic, gilt-edged French mirror reflects almost the whole room.

Few cities in America have protected their historic areas more carefully than Charleston. More than fifty pre-Revolutionary buildings in mint condition exist in the city, but Charleston's particular pride is the nineteenth-century English townhouse architecture that gives the city its distinctive ambience.

The Swordgate Inn has a rack of bicycles for the use of its guests, but it is just as easy to walk around the area. There are forty-nine historic sights listed in the *Chamber of Commerce Visitor's Guide* to the old city; thirty of them are within five blocks of the inn.

Left: The regal entrance to Sword Gate House, after which the inn is named, having once been part of the complex. OVERLEAF: Two views of the elegant ballroom, which is now furnished with additional antiques from the new innkeepers' collection.

SWORDGATE INN, 111 Tradd St., Charleston, S.C. 29401; (803) 723-8518; David and Suzanne Redd, Innkeepers. A 5-room inn located in the heart of Charleston's historic district. Open all year, except Christmas Eve and Day. Single occupancy rate is $48, double $55, triple $75; includes full breakfast. No bar, guests can bring their own. No children under 5, no pets. No credit cards accepted.

DIRECTIONS: Follow the signs to Rutledge Ave. and turn left at Tradd St. The inn is 4 blocks down on the right.

RIVER FOREST MANOR

Belhaven — NORTH CAROLINA

A mansion of grand proportions and eclectic style

River Forest Manor is a turn-of-the-century mansion of grand proportion and complex character. Besides being a wonderful country inn, it is also a fully equipped marina, offers a spectacular smorgasbord nightly, and is furnished from top to bottom in an eclectic mix of periods and tastes.

The mansion was built in 1899 on a shady stretch along the Pungo River by lumber and railroad baron John Aaron Wilkinson, who spared no expense either inside or out. Enamored of elegant European architecture yet unable to decide upon a favorite period, he commissioned Italian artisans to concoct a blend of periods, including an elegant, ionic-columned exterior portico and a Queen Anne-French Provincial-Victorian interior. Leaded, cut glass windows and crystal chandeliers cast rainbows across ornate ceilings; handcarved oak columns and mantles and imported mahogany moldings are displayed throughout.

Within this lovely structure is a cockeyed blend of furnishings that run the gamut from fine antique chests and bedsteads to country crockery lining the formal staircase and a Victorian settee upholstered in vinyl. Guest rooms range from old-fashioned and homey to awe-inspiring. For example, the solarium guest room contains fourteen windows, two Victorian chestnut double beds, and a bathroom so large it easily accommodates a wicker vanity and matching chair beside the free-standing, curl-lipped tub-for-two. The bridal suite features a massive, 200-year-old mahogany canopy bed and an even larger bathroom, complete with two easy chairs, a tub-for-two, and double doors that open onto a mini-balcony overlooking the grand portico and private lawn!

The daily smorgasbord is an institution in its own right. From salad bar to homemade banana ice cream, the display is mind-boggling. Not to be missed are

Left: The entrance hall showing country crockery collection.

Leaded beveled glass and ornate ceiling of the dining room.

the crabmeat casserole—thick with sweet white meat—tangy homemade pickled sausage links, oyster fritters, and tender buttermilk hush puppies slathered with homemade strawberry jam. A wide selection of vegetables, cooked "country style," are grown primarily in the Manor's gardens, and some evenings a cooked-to-order strip steak or succulent soft shell crab is offered along with the already abundant meat dishes.

River Forest Manor was the brainchild of the late Axson Smith, fondly remembered as a "one-man chamber of commerce" who spent a lifetime in the hotel business and had a reputation for enjoying food and lots of it. Today, wife Melba and son Axson, Jr., carry on the tradition of serving up honest American fare in relaxed and congenial surroundings.

RIVER FOREST MANOR, 600 E. Main St., Belhaven, N.C. 27810; (919) 943-2151; Melba Smith and Axson Smith, Jr., Innkeepers. An elegant mansion that pairs a neoclassical exterior with an eclectic mix of interior styles. Open year round. Seven guest rooms, including 3 suites; each guest room has a private bath, 3 with shower only, some with tub only, and some with both. Room rates $29.50 to $39.50; $5 for each additional person, infants free. European plan. Dining room, open to public, serves breakfast and dinner 7 days a week. No bar or lounge, but wine and beer served with dinner. Brown bag license; guests may bring their own wine or liquor for dinner. Children welcome, no pets. MasterCard, Visa, and Texaco credit cards accepted. Hot tub jacuzzi, tennis, boating, fishing, crabbing, bicycle rental on premises; fishing and hunting nearby as well as a museum in town that houses an interesting private collection of early 20th-century oddments.

DIRECTIONS: From Wilmongton, N.C., take Hwy. 17 north to Washington, N.C.; then take Hwy. 264 east to Belhaven. At 1st stoplight take Business 264 to inn, which is 10 blocks ahead on right. From Richmond, Va., take I-95 south to the junction of Hwy. 264; take Hwy. 264 east to Belhaven and follow local directions above.

New Bern ## KINGS ARMS **NORTH CAROLINA**

An elegant inn with three sets of innkeepers

The Kings Arms Inn began when six friends—Walter and Bettye Paramore, Uzie and John Thomas, and Evelyn and John Peterson—started kicking around ideas for a mutual investment. All were interested in preserving one of the old buildings in the downtown area, but none could get excited about their initial idea of opening a dress shop in an historic, but dilapidated, brick house. When they happened upon the gracious frame house on Pollock Street, however, genius stepped in and six innkeepers were born.

With a pooling of talents, restoration and revamping were quickly accomplished. "I wish you could have seen it," said Walter Paramore with a chuckle. "There was the president of a contracting firm (Thomas) hanging a mirror, an architect (Peterson) and a CPA (Paramore) holding the ladder, and the ladies standing back saying 'It's not straight.' " The mirrors, paintings, and curtains did in the end straighten out beautifully, thanks to the ladies who decorated the inn from top to bottom in an elegant combination of Federalist and Empire styles with a dash of Williamsburg.

The inn runs like a top. Due in part to an understanding and cooperative friendship, the real key to success lies in the innkeepers' unique schedule. Each couple takes a turn staying at the inn, one week at a time. There are no innkeepers' quarters; the couple in charge simply check into a guest room, rotating

Tryon Palace.

from room to room, and so becomes familiar with the comforts, and annoyances, of each. By sleeping in one of the front rooms, for example, one couple discovered an intrusive porch light—one that no longer burns at night.

Every morning a breakfast tray laden with ham biscuits and hot blueberry muffins is delivered to each door, accompanied by a silver pot brimming with hot coffee and a copy of the *Raleigh News and Observer*. Other meals can be had two doors down at the Henderson House, which has gained a fine reputation serving lunch from Tuesday through Saturday and dinner on Friday and Saturday nights.

Besides this great little inn, the primary reason to stay in New Bern is to visit the Tryon Palace, which was the residence of the Royal Governor of the colony of North Carolina in 1770 and was then the most beautiful building in America. Breathtakingly perfect in its restored form, this Georgian palace, with its oustanding array of priceless antiques and exquisite formal gardens, rivals in impressiveness colonial Williamsburg.

Left: Formal gardens, above, at Tryon Palace, the prerevolutionary residence of the Royal Governor of North Carolina, now beautifully preserved. Below, a breakfast tray is brought to your room with the morning paper.

KINGS ARMS, 212 Pollock St., New Bern, N.C. 28560; (919) 638-4409; Bettye and Walter Paramore, John and Evelyn Peterson, John and Uzie Thomas, Innkeepers. Colonial frame home dating to the mid-1800s with mansard roof and dormer windows. Open year round. Eleven guestrooms, most with private baths that have facilities for the handicapped; entire 3rd floor can be rented as one unit. Rates from $50 to $55, $5 for extra person, infants free; includes continental breakfast. No restaurant, no bar. Children welcome, no pets. All major credit cards accepted. Nearby golf, swimming, tennis, antique shops, firemen's museum, Tryon Palace.

DIRECTIONS: Take Hwy. 17 to New Bern and turn east on East Front St. and south (right) on Pollock St., where inn is second house on the right.

Rustic hospitality in North Carolina's fabled Outer Banks

A free, forty-minute ferry ride from Hatteras Island on the north—or a toll ferry from Swan Quarter or Cedar Island on the south and west—is the only way, short of a private plane, to reach Ocracoke Island, the middle link in the chain of islands separating the North Carolina mainland and Pamlico Sound from the Atlantic. Nowadays, Ocracoke is home to some 500 residents and several guesthouses, among them the Island Inn.

Operated by Foy Shaw and Larry Williams, whose family goes back to the island's first settlers, the inn is a rustic, unpretentious two-story hostelry that features a two-room crow's nest with cathedral ceilings and a decor essentially unchanged since its last updating in the 1950s. Recent additions to the furnishings include heirloom antiques from Larry's family as well as his extensive and humorous collection of frogs.

The possibilities for dining on the island are few, and the inn's dining room is unchallenged as Ocracoke's leading restaurant. Local specialties on the extensive, well-prepared menu include Ocracoke Clam Chowder, Chicken and Shrimp Ariosto, which is garnished with chopped peanuts, and Stewed Shrimp and Corn Dumplings.

Left: Aerial view of Ocracoke and its sheltered harbor with the Atlantic in the background. OVERLEAF: Atlantic surf breaks in amazing patterns on the sandy beach.

THE ISLAND INN, Box 9, Ocracoke, N.C. 27960; (919) 928-4351; Foy Shaw and Larry Williams, Innkeepers. A rustic, white frame seashore inn with a modern 2-story addition to the original 1901 main house; a cozy, 2-room crow's nest fills the peak of the old building, and second-floor, rocker-filled porch overlooks the bay on the west. Open year round. Thirty-nine rooms, each with private bath (some with shower only). Room rates $26 to $50 in season, $24 to $40 off season (Dec., Jan., Feb.); $3 for each additional person. European plan. Dining room, open to public, serves 3 meals daily 7 days a week in season; off season serves breakfast and dinner only. No bar, but guests may bring wine or liquor to their rooms. Children welcome, no pets. MasterCard, Visa accepted. Piano, board games, television in most rooms; swimming, hiking, nature walks, great fishing, and duck hunting all outside the door. Note that the island has no movie theaters or night life and that in season the mosquitoes can be a real problem.

DIRECTIONS: From Nags Head on the north, take Hwy. 12 to Hatteras Village, where a free ferry runs every 40 min. in season. From the south, drive to Cedar Island, where a toll ferry makes the passage to Ocracoke. Alternatively, from the west take Hwy. 264 to Swan Quarter, which also offers toll-ferry service. Note that there is also an airstrip for the island just outside of town.

FOLKESTONE LODGE

Where dreams come true for the guests and the innkeepers

Interesting inns are operated by interesting people and Folkestone Lodge is no exception. Throughout their married lives Bob and Irene Kranich have worked like demons for six months of the year as engineering draftsmen in order to earn six months "leave"—time to travel through Europe or live off the land by a clear mountain stream. During one six-month stint, they evaluated their harried lives and decided to commit half of each year to life in the mountains. But how to do it? After playing with several ideas, taking into consideration their mutual love for backpacking and Irene's need for hearth and home, they hit upon the perfect solution. Buying an old farmhouse at the southern entrance to the Great Smoky Mountain National Park, the Kranichs set out to become innkeepers.

Pooling their formidable talents and travel experience, the Kranichs created a European farm-style bed-and-breakfast. With a meticulous eye for detail, they transformed the ground floor into a charming and private set of rooms complete with low, pressed-tin ceiling, cobblestone floor, rough-hewn shutters with simple stained glass insets, handmade coverlets, and a wonderful collection of antiques. Upstairs, in the farmhouse proper, two more guest rooms are decorated in "American country," featuring an oak bedroom set, crocheted bedspreads, hooked rugs, and clawfoot bathtubs.

Besides sleeping rooms, the inn offers a comfortable living room with an ornate, wood-burning stove, a well-stocked library supplied with study desk and cards for checking out books, and an airy dining room large enough for the Victorian settee that overlooks the wooden footbridge in front of the inn.

Each morning Irene rises early to begin the morning meal. Although each day's menu differs from the last, a typical breakfast might include a bacon omelet; hot or cold cereal; biscuits, homebaked bread, blueberry muffins, or pancakes; hot, fresh berry cobbler or fresh apple sauce; and grits or fried potatoes. Adequately prepared for a day in the Smokies, guests can wander off on their own or turn to Bob for expert guidance. He operates a guide and outfitting service to accommodate backpackers, hikers, and sportsmen of all ages and levels of experience. He rents equipment, if needed, and provides food, transportation, and experienced advice.

At the Folkestone, combined enthusiasm and professionalism make dreams come true for innkeepers and guests alike.

FOLKESTONE LODGE, Rte. 1, Box 310, Bryson City, N.C. 28713; (704) 488-2730; Irene and Bob Kranich, Innkeepers. Rustic frame cottage with stone foundation and charming country decor. Open June 1 to Oct. 31. Five guestrooms, each has private bath with clawfoot tubs (no showers). Room rates $29 single, $36 double, $9 for each additional child under 16; rates include full country breakfast. Dining room, open to inn guests only, serves large breakfast 7 days a week (no lunch or dinner service); 1 seating for breakfast unless previously arranged. No bar or lounge, but guests may bring their own. Children welcome "in small doses," no pets. MasterCard, Visa accepted. Horseshoes, croquet, ping pong on premises; tennis, swimming, fishing, hiking, craft shops, Smoky Mountain National Park, and Cherokee Indian Reservation nearby.

DIRECTIONS: From Asheville, take I-40 west to Exit 27 (Waynesville/Sylva), which is Rte. 19A/23. Stay in left lane to exit from I-40; missing the exit takes you to Knoxville. Stay on Rte. 19A/23 into Bryson City and then follow green-and-white state signs marking the state's Deep Creek Camp Ground. Lodge is ¼ mi. from park entrance, with a sign on the left indicating the Folkestone's gravel driveway.

Left: The ground-level bathroom with pressed tin ceiling looks out on impatiens flowers blossoming in the garden.

Bryson City # HEMLOCK INN NORTH CAROLINA

Shrug off urban cares in the Smoky Mountains

Built in 1952 in a spectacular setting overlooking the Smoky Mountains, the Hemlock Inn prides itself on having changed little since its opening. The emphasis has always been on rest and relaxation, and to that end there are no phones in the guest rooms nor television in the lobby. Comfortable mountain furniture fills the sprawling structure, and rocking chairs abound on the myriad porches reaching out toward the forested mountain tops. A cozy open hearth flanks one wall of the dining room, inviting guests to pull up an armchair after dinner for a good read from the room's well-stocked library. The adjoining sunporch with floor-to-ceiling windows and a balcony offers yet another spot from which to enjoy the panoramic view and shrug off urban cares.

Ella Jo and John Shell are enthusiastic and very dedicated innkeepers, and they understand the pleasures of eating well. Because some guests stay at the inn for as long as a month or for the entire season, the menu is constantly changing; the food, however, is abundant and carefully prepared. Specialties include coarse ground grits, fresh sausage, curried fruit casserole at breakfast and homemade yeast rolls, banana, apple, okra, or corn fritters, and country fried chicken at dinner.

The native mountain furniture.

Left: From the sunporch on this side of the inn guests have a panoramic view of the Smokies.

HEMLOCK INN, P.O. Drawer EE, Bryson City, N.C. 28713; (704) 488-2885; Ella Jo and John Shell, Innkeepers. An immaculate, board-and-batten mountain lodge with rambling motel-like units, some with private balconies and kitchenettes, all with private baths (4 with showers only). Open May through Oct. Twenty-one guest rooms, including 3 cottages, 2 of which have kitchens. Room rates $42.50 to $61.50 single, $59 to $78 double; $22 for each additional person. Modified American plan, including breakfast and dinner. Dining room, open to public but requiring prior reservation, serves family-style breakfast and dinner 7 days a week. No bar, but guests may bring liquor into their rooms, though not in public rooms. Children welcome, no pets. No credit cards accepted. Ping pong, shuffleboard, skittle, trails on the inn's 65 private acres; Great Smoky Mountain National Park, fishing, hiking, craft shops nearby.

DIRECTIONS: From Asheville, take I-40 west to Exit 27 (Waynesville/Sylva), which is Rte. 19A/23. It is important to stay in left lane to exit from I-40; missing the exit takes you to Knoxville. Inn is 3 miles east of Bryson City, 1 mile off Rte. 19A. The sign indicating the turn-off is in a dairy farm pasture that has 3 silos.

FRYEMONT INN

Bryson City   NORTH CAROLINA

Mountain air; mouth-watering food

Built on a hillside amidst a cover of trees, the Freymont Inn conjures up notions of an elegant, congenial treehouse. The brainchild of lumber baron Amos Frye, the Fryemont Inn was conceived of as the answer to the 1921 failure of his timber business and was designed by Richard Hunt, architect of the Biltmore Estate. The meandering structure is built of the best native wood of the region and is cloaked in unusual, rustic poplar bar shingles. In lobby and dining room enormous rock fireplaces burn seven-foot logs to cool the evening mountain air. And just outside, an open deck with rocking chairs overlooks a pool and tennis courts.

Hearty dining in a pleasant, casual atmosphere can be credited to Catherine Collins, the inn's owner and imaginative chef. From her kitchen issue wonderful treats—among them, mouth-watering breakfast biscuits and for an evening appetizer a Fryemont specialty, delicious cheese soup with vegetables and nuts. Dinner entrées, perhaps succulent country ham or fresh mountain trout, are accompanied by a wealth of fresh, interestingly prepared vegetables and stewed apples, a local dish. The Fryemont's dining room, it should be noted, is one of the few dining establishments in Bryson City and among a handful that serve lunch.

FRYEMONT INN, Box 459, Fryemont Rd., Bryson City, N.C. 28713; (704) 488-2159; Catherine and Jim Collins, Innkeepers. A rustic, 2-story frame and stone lodge with poplar bark siding. Open mid-April to Jan. 1. Thirty-seven rooms, each with its own bath. Room rates for 1982 to be approximately $30 per person, modified American plan. Dining room, requiring reservation, is open to public and serves 7 days a week; weekdays 3 meals a day, Sat. and Sun. no lunch. Wine bar on premises; guests may bring hard liquor or beer for dinner. Children welcome, no pets. MasterCard and Visa accepted. Pool, tennis court, shuffleboard, game tables on premises; craft shops, fishing, hiking, Smoky Mountain National Park.

DIRECTIONS: From Asheville, take I-40 west to Exit 27 (Waynesville/Sylva), which is Rte. 19A/23. It is important to stay in left lane to exit from I-40; missing the exit takes you to Knoxville. Follow Rte. 19A to Bryson City. At courthouse traffic light, turn toward the hill and drive past the police station. At first block (library on corner), turn right and then take the first left onto Fryemont Rd., which leads to the inn's driveway.

The rustic lobby of a mountain lodge.

RANDOLPH HOUSE

Bryson City **NORTH CAROLINA**

Preserves the feeling of a comfortable and charming home

Hemlock pines line the driveway leading up to the gabled, two-story white frame inn, built in 1895 as a home for timber baron and shrewd land title lawyer Amos Frye. An expanse of stone-pillared porch sweeps across the sharply gabled facade; and groves of white oak, maple, and sourwood surround the well-tended lawn and garden. Inside, antiques of varied style and period furnish each of the six guest-rooms and help preserve the feeling of a comfortable and charming home.

"Food is our big drawing card," say innkeepers Bill and Ruth Adams, and no one would argue with them. When making the necessary reservations for dinner, guests are informed of the evening menu and asked at that time to select an entrée. The frequently changing, rather large menu, all expertly prepared by Ruth, might include well-seasoned, fresh mountain trout, stuffed with mushrooms and baked in white wine; or impeccable quail, tender and moist, served with wild rice and pan juices.

THE RANDOLPH HOUSE, Box 16, Fryemont Rd., Bryson City, N.C. 28713; (704) 488-3472; Bill and Ruth Randolph Adams, Innkeepers. A 2-story white frame house with a zig-zag roofline and chunky stone pillars, whose second floor houses 6 guest rooms and 4 baths that must be shared when the inn is full. Open all year long except Thanksgiving Day and Christmas Day. Room rates $32 per person. Modified American plan, with breakfast and dinner included in room rate. Dining room, open to public on a limited basis, requires reservations and advance ordering of dinner selections; breakfast and dinner served 7 days a week. Daily tours at 2 p.m., $1 per person. No bar, but wine can be brought for dinner. Limited acceptance of children, no pets. MasterCard, Visa, and personal checks accepted. Tennis, swimming, fishing, hiking, craft shops, and 2 national parks nearby.

DIRECTIONS: From Ashville, take I-40 west to Exit 27 (Waynesville/Sylva), which is Rte. 19A/23. It is important to stay in the left lane on I-40 to exit; missing the exit takes you to Knoxville! Follow Rte. 19A to Bryson City. At courthouse traffic light, turn toward the hill, driving past the police station; at first block (library on corner), turn right and then take first left onto Fryemont Rd., which takes you to the inn's driveway.

The upstairs hallway, filled with antiques and bric-a-brac.

Tryon # PINE CREST INN **NORTH CAROLINA**

Service you dream of but rarely find

The phrase "simple quality" fits the Pine Crest Inn to a tee. Innkeepers Bob and Fran Hull strive to provide guests with attentive service, and the result is a devoted clientele who return as often as possible.

The Hulls came to innkeeping from Connecticut where Bob commuted to a high-powered job in New York City. "I decided to give it up when I looked around and saw three out of four couples among our friends divorcing." Fran, a registered nurse, had completed her job of rearing the family; so together they embarked on new careers.

The talents Bob developed in the corporate world translated beautifully, making him the consummate innkeeper. Gifted with accurate instincts and a phenomenal memory, Bob gives each guest thoughtful attention. For example, one couple recalls the time their young son left his pajamas at the inn. Time passed. When they returned for their next stay, they found the pajamas washed, pressed, and lying on his bed. That is the kind of service one dreams of but rarely finds. While Bob is out front caring for guests, Fran is in the kitchen concerned with gustatory needs. In charge of preparing three meals a day, seven days a week, she is a talented, energetic, and meticulous chef. A sample from her table might include cheese soufflé with mushroom sauce, curried chicken, and roast duck with cranberry-orange sauce. Breakfast is served with the morning paper, and the service at all meals is strictly professional.

Built in 1906 as a sanitorium and converted in 1917 to an inn, the Pine Crest comprises a main house, offering dining, recreation, and lodging, and a variety of cottages that bear such colorful names as Swayback, Ice Cube, Woodcutter, and Stone House. The main house is furnished with large braided rugs scattered over heart pine floors, overstuffed easy chairs, split-log tables, wrought-iron chandeliers, and

Left: The main lodge viewed from one of the cottages.

Bob and Fran Hull with harvest of perfect peaches from a neighboring orchard.

large open fireplaces. Most of the guest rooms are similarly decorated, and many have working fireplaces that are laid and restocked daily. Set on nine wooded acres, the inn affords a sense of separateness from the world, although, in truth, mountain craft shops, art galleries, and a theater can be found in Tryon's shopping district just several blocks away. To top it off, Tryon is located in the Thermal Belt, protected from northern winds by the southern slope of the Blue Ridge Mountains. Therefore, in addition to good food and genial surroundings, the Pine Crest offers the perfect spot for year-round sports, including golf and hunting and a range of equestrian activities that have made Tryon famous since the 1800s.

PINE CREST INN, Box 1030, Tryon, N.C. 28782; (704) 859-9135; Fran and Bob Hull, Innkeepers. Neoclassical frame main lodge surrounded by stone and log cottages set in the wooded foothills of the Blue Ridge Mountains. Open March 10 to Dec. 13. Three guest rooms and 1 suite in main lodge; 10 guesthouses, varying from single suites to accommodations for as many as 6; all rooms have private baths with tub and shower. Room rates available upon request; gratuity added to bill for dining room and maid service. European plan. Dining room, open to public but reservation mandatory; serves 3 meals daily. No bar or lounge, but wine is available at dinner and guests may bring their own wine or liquor. Children welcome, no pets. No credit cards. Personal checks, traveler's checks accepted, or bill can be sent. Hiking, horseback riding, golf, tennis, swimming, mountain craft shops, theater, Carl Sandburg home, Biltmore House, and textile factory outlets nearby.

DIRECTIONS: From Asheville, N.C., take I-26 south to the Columbus Exit (Rte. 108) and stay on Rte. 108 into Tryon. At the railroad tracks, instead of crossing them, bear left up the hill on New Market Rd. At top of hill, take first left after Methodist Church, which is Pine Crest Lane and leads to the inn.

JARRETT HOUSE

Dillsboro

Fresh country food prepared by local mountain women

"We have acquired a legend," explain Jim and Jean Hartbarger, owners since 1975 of the Jarrett House, and they intend to uphold it. Built in 1884 by William Allen Dills, founder of the town of Dillsboro, the Jarrett House then served as official dining stopover for the noon arrival of the passenger train from Asheville. As the town quickly grew into a summer resort, the inn's clientele expanded steadily and so too did its reputation for excellent home-style food.

"Today," laughs Jim, "some people say we serve it faster than McDonalds." Fast the service may be, but at no expense to the palate. Insistent upon maintaining the high quality upon which the inn's reputation is built, the Hartbargers avoid advertising altogether, fearing that excess demand will inevitably affect quality. Prepared by local mountain women,

the food is fresh, hot, abundant, and very reasonably priced. Dinner specialties include excellent southern fried chicken, fresh mountain trout, and truly fine country cured ham, all served with delicious buttery biscuits, cole slaw, and baked "candied" apples. Hot berry cobbler and delicious vinegar pie are special desserts—provided you can find room!

JARRETT HOUSE, Box 219, Dillsboro, N.C. 28725; (704) 586-9964; Jim and Jean Hartbarger, Innkeepers. This 3-story, white frame structure with ornate wrought-iron porch rails has a pleasant, simple decor that provides a backdrop for the inn's main feature—its food. Open April 1 to Nov. 1. Twenty antique-filled rooms, each with private bath. Room rates $25 single, $28 double; $3 for each additional person. European plan. Dining room, open to public, serves 3 meals a day 7 days a week. No bar, but guests may bring wine or beer for dinner. Children over 12 welcome, no pets. No credit cards; personal checks are accepted. Nice craft and clothing shops around the corner; fishing, rafting, canoeing, hiking nearby. A visit to see the fall foliage will prove a real treat.

DIRECTIONS: From Asheville, take I-40 west to Exit 27 (Waynesville/Sylva), which is Rte. 19A/23. Stay in left lane to exit from I-40; if you miss the exit, you will end up in Knoxville. Follow Rte. 19A/23 to Dillsboro, where the inn is on Main St.

The slow-paced mountain town of Dillsboro, showing the inn at the end of the road.

A mountain resort with lots to do

Nestled in the Cashiers Valley of the Blue Ridge Mountains, High Hampton Inn was built over a century ago as a summer home for South Carolina's illustrious General Wade Hampton. In the 1890s famed Johns Hopkins surgeon William Halsted and his wife, Caroline, General Hampton's niece, purchased the 2300-acre estate and lovingly landscaped it, adding the famous Halsted dahlia garden. In 1922 the parents of present innkeeper William McKee acquired the property and converted it into an inn.

   Built in a stunning mountain setting at the edge of a lake and forests, High Hampton is a masterly blend of rustic and elegant with a chestnut bark exterior; massive four-sided fireplace in the lobby; decor that combines upholstery with sturdy, handmade mountain furniture; seven tennis courts; large vegetable garden, which contributes nightly to the evening

meal; and an 18-hole golf course designed by George W. Cobb. For children there is a busy program of daily activities and crafts, and for adults any number of sports and things to do. Special events, including golf clinics, holiday weekends, and summer equitation school, are regular features of High Hampton. Although by its very size High Hampton does not strictly qualify as a country inn, it is a fine example of a particular breed of resort popular in this region.

HIGH HAMPTON INN, Box 338, Cashiers, N.C. 28717; (704) 743-2411; William D. McKee, Innkeeper. A very rustic, yet elegant mountain lodge set on a rambling 2300-acre estate that boasts an 18-hole golf course, man-made lake, tennis courts, stables, gardens, and the beauty of the Blue Ridge Mountains in the background. Open April 1 to Nov. 1. Guest rooms number 132, with 14 cabins; all have private baths with shower and tub. Room rates in season (July 1 through Aug. 31) $43.50 to $48.50 double, $50.50 to $52.50 single; off season $41 to $45 double, $47 to $50 single; extra person in room $28.50 in season, $25.50 off season; child under 6 in room with 2 adults $24 in season, $22 off season. Rates are based upon 7-day stay, with $2.75 additional daily fee per person for shorter visits; discount available for month-long off-season stay. Full American plan includes 3 meals daily. Dining room, open to public, serves 3 meals daily 7 days a week. Lounge with entertainment furnishes drink setups but by N.C. law cannot sell liquor; guests may bring their own. Children welcome. No credit cards accepted; checks accepted or bill sent to home address. Golf, tennis, swimming, sailing, canoeing, trout fishing, nature walks, horseback riding, extensive children's program, separate teenagers' club room, trap and skeet shooting, climbing, hiking, leathercraft classes, equitation school in summer.
   DIRECTIONS: From Asheville, take I-26 south to Hendersonville and then Hwy. 64 west to Brevard and Cashiers. At the intersection of Hwy. 64 and State Rd. 107, follow 107 south 2 mi. to the inn's entrance.

The guest rooms are primly comfortable.

OVERLEAF: The green of the par 3 eighth hole juts out into the lake, making a frightening golf shot for duffers.

A fine old family inn made for relaxation

Commanding Burnsville's village square is the Nu-Wray Inn, a landmark in Burnsville since 1867, when Garrett T. Ray first expanded an old eight-room log cabin and turned it into Ray's Inn. Mr. Ray's daughter Julia married William Wray, and in 1917 they took over after renaming the inn. Change, however, comes slowly in the Smoky Mountains, and there are still a few old-timers in the area who refer to the Nu-Wray Inn as "the new Wray place in the old Ray place."

By whatever name, it is a big, comfortable three-story country house that has been providing down-home hospitality for more than one hundred years. When innkeeper Rush Wray and his sister Annie Wray Bennett summon guests for dinner, it is time for some fancy country eating. As many as twenty dishes are served on the three long tables in the dining room, where everybody eats family-style. The house specialty is smoked, cured ham dipped in a sauce of molasses, brown sugar and red pepper. There are piles of chicken with cornbread stuffing and milk gravy; sweet and sour beef stew; baked beans; candied yams; and bowls of such locally grown vegetables as summer squash, turnip greens, tomatoes, corn on the cob and snap beans. Annie Wray Bennett makes stacks of biscuits served with fresh, country butter. People have been raving about them for years, and she doesn't understand why. "They're just plain old homemade biscuits," she protests.

The Nu-Wray is a house that loves music. Instead of using the traditional dinner bell to announce supper, Rush plays a tune on a German-built Regi-naphone music box. During the meal, he sets the Steinway Duo-Art player piano in the music room to work playing piano rolls of every form of music, from jazz and honky-tonk to Liszt and Chopin.

The furnishings at the Nu-Wray are good, solid country pieces, with the emphasis on comfort rather than on great style. The downstairs sitting room is very relaxing, with an oversized stone fireplace at one end and a particularly fine deacon's chair with patchwork pillows. Daniel Boone VII, a direct descendant, made the ironwork for the fireplace and the overhead lighting fixtures, as well. The room also houses charming collections of corn-husk dolls, quilts and pillows made by the local women.

NU-WRAY INN, Box 156, Burnsville, N.C. 28714; (704) 682-2329; Rush Wray, Manager, Howard and Betty Souders, Inkeepers. A 35-room inn located on the town square. Open all year, but the kitchen closes from Dec. to May. Single occupancy rates range from $20 to $22, double $32 to $35; $5 for extra person; some rooms share baths. Restaurant, open to public, serves breakfast and dinner, Sunday luncheon. No bar. Children welcome, no pets. Weekly rates, including all meals, are available by prior arrangement. No credit cards accepted. State Park, Blue Ridge Mountains, Biltmore Estate nearby.

DIRECTIONS: From Asheville, take U.S.-19 north to Burnsville. The inn is located in the center of town on the square.

Left: A grand old 1930s Stromberg-Carlson radio. OVER-LEAF: An intricately carved Black Forest cuckoo clock is part of a collection amassed over the years. Right, above, is the town square showing General Burns, the big man in town, and the inn at left. Below is the country store on the other side of the square. It has 14 rooms stuffed with exotic goods for sale.

Abingdon MARTHA WASHINGTON INN

A Southern mansion in the grand style

A circular drive, bordered by roses, sweeps up to the door of the massive, three-section Federalist mansion; the first impression is one of elegance and sheer size. The original center section of The Martha, as it is dubbed locally, was built in 1832 as a private residence and then for nearly seventy-five years served as home to the Martha Washington College for women before finally becoming a country inn.

A lovely, high-ceilinged foyer with a gracefully curved staircase and cherry bannister welcomes arriving guests, and its petticoat mirror introduces the inn's impressive collection of antiques. Whether a rare eighteenth-century burled walnut grandfather clock, a nineteenth-century English partners' desk, or an ornately carved canopy bed, visual treats abound throughout the inn for the antique aficionado. It should be noted that considerable renovation is underway, with most, but not all, guest rooms now redecorated.

The menu in the inn's restaurant is extensive and changes seasonally, and the newly expanded lounge features live music and dancing twice weekly.

MARTHA WASHINGTON INN, 150 West Main St., Abingdon, Va. 24210; (703) 628-3161; Ellison Ketchum, General Manager. An elegant Federalist mansion with Georgian accents that cannot help but remind visitors of the plantation in *Gone With the Wind*. Open all year. Eighty rooms, including 8 suites, all with private baths (some with tubs only). Room rates $50 single, $60 double, $85 to $125 suites; children under 12 free. Dining room open to public, serving 3 meals daily, 7 days a week; bar and lounge open nightly, with live music and dancing Tuesdays and Saturdays. No pets. All major credit cards except Carte Blanche. Shuffleboard, badminton, horseshoes, and croquet on grounds; excellent craft shops in area; the Barter Theatre, a professional repertory company open from April to October, just across the street; golf, tennis, swimming, hiking, ski resorts, and national recreation area nearby.

DIRECTIONS: From Roanoke, Va., or from Knoxville, Tenn., take I-81 to Exit 8 (Abingdon); drive 1 mile into town and turn right on Main Street. Inn is on the right.

Left: Afternoon tea is served daily on the grand porch.

WAYSIDE INN

Middletown

VIRGINIA

Colonial dining in the Shenandoah Valley

Given its present name in 1908, the Wayside Inn is now one of the most famous tourist accommodations in the Shenandoah Valley, a comfortable blend of the old and the new where expanded facilities for large groups complement the centuries-old original structure.

The old slave kitchen with its gigantic open-hearth fireplace is a charming brick-faced dining room, and the coach yard has been transformed into a cocktail lounge. The rooms in the original building have kept the old, quirky individuality that was common in the days when overnight lodgings were created by craftsmen and not computers.

Today we tend to think of "Early American" as a rigidly maintained style where every piece of furniture in the house came from the same period. In the eighteenth century, of course, there was no such thing as an Early American style. The Virginians of that day gladly mixed their heirlooms from England with their own locally made chairs, tables, cabinets and beds. And those lucky enough to acquire Oriental furniture, bric-a-brac and ornaments that resulted from the China Trade displayed them proudly in their homes. Present-day visitors to the Wayside Inn will find a delightful commingling of American, English and Chinese antiques.

The Wayside Inn sets a good Virginia table, which means that its menu is rich with locally produced meats, poultry and vegetables. Its apple juice, which has been the pride of Virginia for two hundred years, comes right from the Shenandoah Valley, as do its hams, which are all country-cured and processed by neighboring farmers. The distinctive Virginia ham is

The inn stands directly on the roadside, where this sign catches the traveler's eye.

one of those happy culinary accidents of the New World. In the middle of the seventeenth century, English piglets let loose on the Virginia countryside began to fatten themselves on local products, especially wild peanuts, which eventually gave the local ham its unique flavor. As with many of the traditional regional dishes served at the Wayside Inn, the hams are prepared according to eighteenth-century recipes: they are soaked overnight and then cooked with dark molasses for extra flavor.

WAYSIDE INN SINCE 1797, 7783 Main St., Middletown, Va. 22645; (703) 869-1797; Margie Alcarese, Innkeeper. A 21-room inn located in the Shenandoah Valley. Open all year. Room rates $50 to $100; all rooms have private baths, 2 rooms have working fireplaces. Restaurant, open to public, daily serves breakfast, lunch and dinner. Bar open daily. Children welcome, no pets. American Express, MasterCard and Visa accepted.

DIRECTIONS: From Washington, D.C., take I-66 west to I-81; go north on I-81 and take exit 77 into Middletown. The inn is located in the center of town.

Left: Early in America's national history, this dining room served travelers on the Shenandoah Valley Turnpike.

Middleburg # RED FOX TAVERN **VIRGINIA**

Thomas Jefferson stopped here

The Red Fox Tavern has been part of American social history ever since it served its first tankard of ale in 1728. George Washington surveyed the land and Thomas Jefferson stopped here on his journeys between Monticello and the White House. During the Civil War, the tavern was often used as a Confederate headquarters. Colonel John Mosby and his irregulars planned many of their devastating guerrilla raids here.

By the mid-1970s, the Red Fox had been through some hard times and had gone to seed. Fortunately, it was bought in 1976 by the energetic Nancy Brown Reuter, a busy Virginia lady with many interests who calls herself the "smallest living conglomerate in the world." Mrs. Reuter and her daughter Diana, a noted interior designer, set to work restoring the Red Fox to its colonial splendor. They went to the restoration at Williamsburg and brought back traditional wallpapers, bedspreads and patterns. They brought antiques from their own home and polished the old place up until it was as bright and shiny as it had been in Jefferson's day. The six upstairs bedrooms are warm and cozy, with braided rugs and patterned wallpapers. Five of the rooms are fitted out with four-poster canopied beds and have their own fireplaces.

The main dining room is a classic country restaurant setting with a low, beamed ceiling and freshly painted, white stone walls. "We have cooks, not chefs," says Mrs. Reuter. "We don't try to be a French restaurant." The menu at the Red Fox tends toward solid country food: Brunswick stew, crab cakes, country ham with red-eye gravy and fresh fish. For special parties, the Red Fox will prepare a game dinner of quail, venison, pheasant and duck.

In back of the Red Fox there is a separate cottage known as the Night Fox, where the beat picks up appreciably. It is a combination restaurant and bar much favored by the younger crowd who like their music with charcoal-broiled hamburgers and french fries. The music may be a bit different now but the spirit of conviviality is much as it was 250 years ago, when prosperous Virginia planters would stop by to enjoy themselves.

RED FOX TAVERN, 2 E. Washington St., Middleburg, Va. 22117; (703) 687-6301; Turner Reuter, Innkeeper. A 6-room inn in the Virginia foxhunting country. Open all year. Room rates range from $55 to $85. Restaurant, open to public, provides elegant dining in 18th-century setting; serves 3 meals daily, reservations recommended. Bar open daily. Children welcome, no pets. Visa, MasterCard, American Express accepted.

DIRECTIONS: From Washington, D.C., take I-66 west to Rte. 50; go west on Rte. 50 to Middleburg, where inn is located in center of town.

The guest rooms are sumptuous, with braided rugs and canopied bedsteads. OVERLEAF: The furnishings of two of the dining rooms show the graceful strength of colonial Virginia furniture.

A wonderful place to get reacquainted

"Usually on trips we stay at a motel. We walk into the room and first thing turn on the television," says one couple who recently stayed at the Hotel Strasburg. "But here we took a walk through town and spent an evening getting to know each other again." A charming, genteel, and relaxed small-town hotel set in the lovely Shenandoah Valley, the Strasburg is a wonderful place to get reacquainted.

Built in the 1890s as a private hospital, the hotel was converted to an inn in 1915; it has since been enlarged and recently underwent head-to-toe reno-vation to restore it to its original Victorian elegance. Greeted by a lobby decorated with Oriental rugs, Victorian velvet settees, and myriad prints and paint-ings, guests sign in at an old-fashioned check-in desk bedecked with fresh flowers. Adjoining the lobby is the Depot Lounge, a bar with exquisite Tiffany-style lamps, a collection of model trains, a wood-burning stove, and the hotel's sole TV. The guest rooms, all decorated in a different color scheme, are likewise furnished with antiques, and several are favorites, including Rooms 1 and 8.

In the dining room, filled with oak tables and fresh flowers, the simple menu features home cooking. The soups are legendary, and among the entrées succulent pan-fried chicken with a corn-meal crust is excellent. A nice addition to each meal is a loaf of hot bread and delicious, homemade apple butter.

HOTEL STRASBURG, 201 Holliday St., Strasburg, Va. 22657; (703) 465-9191; Andrew Hayes, Innkeeper. A turn-of-the-century, mansard-roofed frame inn, set in the heart of the Shenandoah Valley. Open year round. Seventeen guest rooms, including 3 private suites with private baths; 14 rooms share baths. Room rates $20 to $40 single, $25 to $45 double; rates include continental breakfast in dining room. Restaurant, open to public, serves 3 meals daily. Weekdays, continental breakfast; weekends, full complete breakfast. Bar on premises. Children welcome, pets wel-come. American Express, MasterCard, Visa accepted. No recreational facilities on grounds; nearby are Shenandoah vineyards, Strasburg Railway Museum, George Washing-ton's headquarters, Civil War memorabilia, antique shops, golf, and Wayside Wonderland, a quarry with beach and boating available to public.

DIRECTIONS: From Washington, D.C., take I-66 west to I-81 and south on I-81 to Strasburg Exit 75. Go south on Rte. 11 approximately 1½ miles to 1st traffic light. Turn right one block, then left at the light (Holliday St.). Inn is located 1 block down on the left.

A stained glass window in the bar.

The main attraction of Chesapeake House is the cooking.

An island inn with seafood specialties

"Keep everything good, and they'll keep coming back," say Chesapeake House innkeepers Bette Nohe and Edna Moore. Theirs is a concise philosophy, in effect and clearly working since the inn was opened in 1940 by Hilda Crockett, Bette and Edna's mother. In 1974 the two sisters took over the inn after their mother's death but changed little, if anything—certainly not Hilda's recipes that have delighted innumerable diners over the years and gained considerable repute.

The Chesapeake House is, in fact, two houses, the original main house and, directly across the road, a second house that was bought in 1966. Both over a century old, the houses are typical Eastern Shore clapboard structures. "Nothing fancy about the inn," cautions Bette, "just two big, old homes—nice and clean and comfortable."

Food is the big drawing card at Chesapeake House, which is the island's only hotel and restaurant. The family-style menu features hearty, homecooked food, including Tangier Island crab cakes, clam fritters, baked Virginia ham, hot corn pudding, all-butter pound cake, and a bottomless 30¢ cup of coffee. Breakfast and dinner are served in the family-style dining room; lunch must be had in one of the island's numerous sandwich shops.

"There's absolutely nothing to do on this island," laughs Bette, "but relax." And a steady stream of guests arrives year after year to do just that.

The inn was painted red, white, and blue in 1976.

CHESAPEAKE HOUSE, Tangier Island, Va. 23440; (804) 891-2331; Bette Nohe and Edna Moore, Innkeepers. Two comfortable, simply appointed clapboard houses, both over a century old, on this island in the middle of the Chesapeake Bay. Open April 1 to Nov. 1. Nine guestrooms, which share 3 bathrooms. Room rates $22 per person, includes full breakfast and family-style dinner. Dining room, open to public, serves 2 meals daily. No bar or lounge. Children welcome, no pets. No credit cards. Swimming, fishing, nature walks.

DIRECTIONS: From Reedville, Va., Tangier Island Cruises provides daily boat service to the island, departing at 10 AM; the 2-hr. crossing costs approximately $16. There is also boat service from Crisfield, Md., on the daily 12:30 PM mail boat, which also charges about $16. As well, Tangier Island has a small airport for private planes.

Warm Springs INN AT GRISTMILL SQUARE

Superlative food and healing waters

Virginia's picturesque mountains and mineral springs have attracted pilgrims since the 1700s. Those fortunate enough to escape the doldrums have fled to the healing waters, sheltered in cool and fragrant mountain valleys. Today Warm Springs continues to offer up its clear and sulphurous bounty just one mile down a country road from the Inn at Gristmill Square.

According to veteran innkeepers Jack and Janice McWilliams, the Gristmill is not exactly a country inn. It is really an historic commercial site meticulously converted into a small village square. The focal point is an old mill built along the crystal clear Warm Springs Run, which remains, as Thomas Jefferson described it, "a very bold stream, sufficient to work a gristmill." Housed inside the mill is the Waterwheel Restaurant whose food is superlative. Lunch and dinner are served six days a week, and specialties include smoked boneless mountain trout served with horseradish in fresh whipped cream, escargots marinated in wine and baked in herbed garlic butter, sautéed chicken baked in a mushroom and tarragon cream sauce, a special veal dish, and tender barbecued baby spareribs bathed in tangy sauce. Dinner arrives with a hot loaf of Janice's wonderful bread, and, if waistline and conscience permit, you might cap it off with a Little Mountain, a treat of rum ice cream and fresh summer fruits topped with meringue and toasted almonds, or a frozen Amaretto soufflé.

The guest rooms are situated both within the square and in a small cottage, dubbed the Quilt Room House, across the lane. Accommodations range from the traditionally furnished and spacious Silo Suite with its circular living room, sundeck, fully equipped kitchen, two bedrooms, two baths, and a washer and dryer, to the Board Room, which is a comfortable bed-sitting room dressed in rough barnsiding with a wide plank floor.

The square contains a general store which is filled with kitchenware, gifts of all types, and imported foods and beverages; an art gallery specializing in paintings, prints, and one-of-a-kind clothing; three tennis courts, and a swimming pool. The town of Warm

The general store and the Silo suite.

Springs is minute, with the current population standing at 320; yet it boasts several impressive churches, a massive turn-of-the-century courthouse, and a lovely antique shop.

Just down the road in Hot Springs resides the famed Homestead. Gristmill guests may partake of resort facilities, including golf, fishing, riding, skeet shooting, the spas, and dining.

THE INN AT GRISTMILL SQUARE, Box 359, Warm Springs, Va. 24484; (703) 839-2231; Janice and Jack McWilliams, Innkeepers. Historic site converted into a small village square with various buildings, including the inn's guest rooms and a restored mill that houses the inn restaurant. Open year round, except for 2 weeks in March. Six units, including 2 apartments with 2 bedrooms each, and 2/2-room suites; each unit has private bath, most have working fireplaces. Rates $50 to $57 apartment, $46 to $52 suite, $8 for additional person; includes continental breakfast. Restaurant, open to public, serves lunch and dinner 6 days a week. Bar on premises. Children, pets welcome. All major credit cards accepted. Tennis courts, swimming pool, country store, art gallery in square; fishing, golf, riding, spas nearby.

DIRECTIONS: From Staunton, Va., take Rte. 254 to Buffalo Gap and then Rte. 42 to Millboro Spring and Rte. 39 to Warm Springs. From Roanoke, take I-81 north to Lexington and then Rte. 39 to Warm Springs. From Richmond, take Rte. 60 to Lexington and then Rte. 39 to Warm Springs.

Left: The old gristmill houses the Waterwheel Restaurant.

COUNTRY INN

Berkeley Springs   **WEST VIRGINIA**

The comfortable living room.

A charming inn at America's oldest spa

Berkeley Springs, in West Virginia, is the oldest spa in America. George Washington happened upon its mineral springs in 1748 and enjoyed their healing properties so much he built a summer home here after his return from the Revolution in 1784.

One of the landmarks of Berkeley Springs is the Country Inn, built in 1933, just a few yards from the original spring. The present owners, Jack and Adele Barker, first came to the Country Inn as guests in the early 1970s. Adele was recuperating from an accident; Jack was a retired schoolmaster. They spent an entire summer at the inn, and when it was up for sale in 1972, Jack decided to step out of retirement and "start perking again."

The inn is a solid, three-story house with six white pillars in front that give a somewhat formal look to the establishment. Actually, it is a charmingly furnished country home built for comfort and filled with family touches the Barkers brought with them. Jim is a deft maker of collages; several examples of his handiwork, combining musical instruments with old musical scores, are around the house. The dining room is a high-ceilinged room with white walls dramatically highlighted by dark wood paneling. Running around the entire circumference of the room is a single shelf of antiques and assorted knickknacks, including clocks, coffee tins, pitchers, baskets and tea kettles. The inn specializes in down-home country cooking and serves three hefty meals a day. The

Berkeley Room downstairs is a large open area used for card games and general recreation.

Although all the standard resort-type attractions are in the area, such as golf, tennis, hunting and fishing, the springs are the principal attraction. The health spa is operated by the state. In addition to enjoying the famous spring waters, guests can get a massage and mineral bath for less than ten dollars a day.

Left: Kevin, son of manager William North, dressed for the winter weather. OVERLEAF: The Berkeley Room provides the setting for an exciting game of bridge.

THE COUNTRY INN, 207 South Washington St., Berkeley Springs, W. Va. 25411; (304) 258-2210; Jack and Adele Barker, Innkeepers. A 37-room inn located next to the Berkeley Mineral Springs State Park. Open all year. Room rates $28 to $38, some with shared baths; Master rooms $42 to $45; suites $50 to $55; $5 for extra person. Restaurant, open to public, serves 3 meals daily and features new garden terrace dining with dancing on weekends. Children and pets welcome. American Express, MasterCard and Visa credit cards accepted. Two state parks nearby.

DIRECTIONS: From Washington, D.C., take I-70 west to Hancock, Md., and then Rte. 522 south 5 mi. to Berkeley Springs. The inn is located on Rte. 522, adjacent to the state park.

A mixed bag of charming treasures

The lobby of the General Lewis Inn spells charm: hardwood floors, cloaked in lovely oriental rugs; exposed beam ceiling; horsehair settees; a trio of rocking chairs pulled invitingly up to the fireplace; and a wonderful collection of china filling corner cupboards. Just beyond the lobby is Museum Hall with a fascinating assembly of guns, tools, musical instruments, kitchen utensils, and other nineteenth-century artifacts. The guest rooms, furnished in a mixed bag of treasures that might feature a massive sleigh bed or cannonball four-poster, are a bit dowdy but nonetheless quite comfortable and pleasant.

Although food at the General Lewis is perfectly adequate, the simple country menu is not particularly imaginative and is definitely secondary to the decor. Operated continuously under the same ownership since 1929, the General Lewis is a great place to stay while enjoying golf and dining at the Greenbrier just a short drive away.

GENERAL LEWIS INN, Lewisburg, W. Va. 24901; (304) 645-2600; Col. Charles May, General Manager. A plantation-style mansion that features a wonderful collection of antiques and a lovely, shaded veranda and garden. Open year round. All 27 rooms, including 2 suites, have private baths with shower and tub. Room rates $25 single; $30 double; $35 to $45 master room with 2 double beds; $45 to $55 suites with 3 double beds. During state fair week, modified American plan, including breakfast and dinner buffet, available; otherwise European plan. Dining room, open to public, serves 7 days a week; closed Christmas Day. No bar yet, though one is planned; guests may bring wine for dinner. Children welcome, extra charge for pets. Visa, MasterCard, and American Express accepted. Antique shows, livestock sales in surrounding area; golf at nearby Greenbrier, swimming at local country club. Nearby attractions include Organ Cave; Lost World Caverns; and New River Gorge Bridge, the world's longest steel arch bridge.

DIRECTIONS: From Charleston, W. Va., take I-64 to Rte. 219 and drive into Lewisburg. At Washington St., turn left and drive 2 blocks to inn on the right.

A crocheted canopy caps a four poster in one of the guest rooms.